"This wonderful resource provides a rich variety of activities exactly suited to the young child. The instructions for the teacher are clear; the materials are inexpensive and readily available; and the content and activities for each subject are very well developed. The model of a hub (central theme) and spokes (multisensory activities) provides a great deal of flexibility that allows teachers to use these activities with their classroom textbook. This flexibility also makes this a valuable resource for vacation/summer programs. I am especially impressed with the work the author has done with the music and book suggestions and the parent pages. Bravissimo!"

Bill Krumm, M.A.
Archdiocese of Cincinnati Early Childhood Advisory Committee

150 Activities to Enrich
Religion Classes
for Young Children

CAROLE MacCLENNAN

TWENTY-THIRD PUBLICATIONS
Mystic, Connecticut 06355

Twenty-Third Publications
185 Willow Street
P.O. Box 180
Mystic CT 06355
(203) 536-2611
800-321-0411

ISBN 0-89622-562-3
Library of Congress Catalog Card Number 92-60026

To the memory of my mother and father

CONTENTS

Each of these chapters contains the following sections: Discussion, Discovery Centers, Crafts, Movement, Prayer, Music, Books, Parent Page

LEARNING BY DOING

INTRODUCTION

This book is intended for busy catechists who need to find and execute ideas quickly, and for children who learn by experiencing. It was inspired by a catechist who, after politely sitting through most of a classroom management lecture I was giving, raised her hand and said in a near-panic voice, "I'm teaching 'Family' next week, and I don't know what to *do*. My text says to draw and color and we're all tired of that. What can I do?"

Because that question is a common one, and because children learn by using all their senses, this book suggests things "to do" to supplement existing curricula. Its goal is to offer a variety of ideas that will support the subject matter, sequenced lesson plans, and thematic stories found in many early childhood and primary religious education textbooks.

The format suggests looking at each lesson as a wheel. Think of the story or truth to be taught as the hub, or center, of your lesson. The spokes that radiate from the hub are the activities that enable the students to experience the central theme. Both the hub and the spokes are necessary to support the rim, which is your completed lesson. Just as the wheel needs all its spokes to be strong, so, too, your lesson needs a number of activities to be educationally strong. The basis for this is that children learn best when they can experience many short activities that support the same theme.

Each chapter in this book, then, revolves around a topic commonly found in young children's religious education texts. The chapters are divided into eight spokes, or supporting members. These are Discussion, Discovery Centers, Crafts, Movement, Prayer, Music, Books, and Parent Page. Each spoke suggests sensory activities or resources that support the topic, or thematic center. A catechist can choose one or more activities from any or all of the spokes to enrich a particular lesson. By using at least one of the activities from each lesson, the catechist would build a complete "lesson wheel."

Here are the parts, or spokes, you'll find in each part of the "lesson wheel":

DISCUSSION

This includes teacher background and sample questions that might be used for discussion starters. In the discussion, talk about the children's own experiences and connect their experiences with God's teaching. Ask questions that require thinking, rather than only a "yes" or "no" answer. Your interest in and acceptance of their answers will make the children feel comfortable enough to share their thoughts.

DISCOVERY CENTER

This spoke contains a list of performance objectives, materials, and procedures for self-directed activities. The performance objectives are listed first so that teachers can decide quickly (without having to read through materials and procedures lists) whether or not the suggested activity matches the teaching goals. When necessary, teacher preparation is noted in the "procedure" section before directions for the children are given. The discovery center activities focus on student self-discovery of the lesson's theme. Students can use these centers with minimal explanation and guidance by the teacher. Make these centers available for use as students arrive in the room and for the first few minutes of class.

CRAFTS

This part lists performance objectives, materials, and procedures for simple things children can make. To encourage creativity and a sense of accomplishment, keep craft projects simple so that the children can do most of the work themselves. (Pre-cutting is usually necessary for young students.)

MOVEMENT

Ideas for non-competitive games, finger-plays, stretching exercises, action songs, and creative dramatics are given here. Emphasis in these activities is placed on children having fun together rather than competing against each other. In class, alternate these "movement" times with "quiet sitting" times.

PRAYER

Suggestions for a prayer activity, a response prayer, and a simple teacher-led "repeat prayer" are offered in this section. Include prayer in every lesson. Make it a welcome and natural thing. Create opportunities for children to experience prayer in many different ways. Speak, think, sing, or dance prayer. Stand, sit, kneel, hold hands, lift up arms, or fold hands together. Pray spontaneously, pray a response in unison, or repeat teacher-led prayer. Send prayer suggestions home.

MUSIC

Titles of recorded songs and their sources are listed in this spoke. Play music as children enter the room and during craft time. Sing along, clap, dance, or march to specific songs during class when appropriate. Borrow music from a library or from the office of religious education.

BOOKS

This spoke contains a bibliography of picture books and easy readers. Set up a comfortable, welcoming book corner and use it as a discovery center or as a place where children can go when they have finished a task. Read specific books when appropriate during a lesson. Borrow books from a library. Give parents suggestions for books they can read with their children during the week to develop the lesson at home.

PARENT PAGE

Because many textbooks already include letters to parents, this part offers suggestions for simple activities that parents can do at home for or with their children to live out and develop the lesson taught in class. Also included in this spoke is an appropriate Bible verse or inspirational quotation that could be passed on to parents. The Parent Pages may be duplicated and distributed to the students' parents.

These eight parts, or spokes, of the "lesson wheel" contain suggestions that are meant to keep your lesson rolling and to set your own creative "wheels" in motion!

Build your own music and book lists, exchange ideas with other catechists. If some of the activities are too difficult or too easy for your particular group, feel free to change and improve them.

Take advantage of the ample white space throughout this book to record your ideas, lists, and evaluations. May these "lesson wheels" help to carry your students closer to the Lord!

CHAPTER 1   # SPECIAL ME

Discussion

BACKGROUND

Many early childhood curricula begin with a lesson on the subject most important to a child: "me!" Children at this age are busy discovering what their bodies can do and how they fit in with the world around them. Slowly, they come to see themselves as individuals and develop a sense of self-esteem. This is a critical process, because self-esteem affects all we do: how we work, play, and relate to others, how we think, learn, and make choices.

Children with high self-esteem feel capable and lovable and are inclined to become successful and loving. Believing they are unique and wonderful will help them to believe that "God made us and we are good." Children who value themselves will value others. They'll be able to accept individual differences, build healthy relationships, and offer understanding and love to others.

Adults can nurture the growth of positive self-esteem by helping children to set realistic goals, giving honest praise, encouraging them to try new things, listening to them, calling them by name lovingly, and loving and valuing them for themselves.

QUESTIONS

Who has brown eyes? blue eyes? green eyes? brown hair? blond hair? black hair? red hair? What do you like about the way you look?

Who in this room looks exactly like you?

Why do you think God made everyone different? (Tell them God wanted someone exactly like each of them. Even though God made everyone different, God loves everyone equally.)

What is something that you can do now that you couldn't do when you were a baby?

What is something you are just learning to do?

What is something you do well?

What is something you like to do more than anything else?

Discovery Centers
"I Can" Box

CHILDREN WILL

>snap, zip, button, buckle, or lace
>feel a variety of objects
>accomplish a task
>feel good about mastering a skill
>learn they can do many things

MATERIALS

>A large box containing things to snap, zip, button, buckle, lace

PROCEDURE

>Choose an object to work with. Complete the task. Take apart so the next person can use it. Work with as many things as time permits.

Guess the Special Person

CHILDREN WILL

>see own reflection in mirror
>identify self as "special"
>experience being valued for self

MATERIALS

>Medium-sized box, small mirror, wrapping paper, glue, tape, scissors, markers, glitter

PROCEDURE

>(Teacher preparation: Cover box. Cut a 5" diameter circle in the front of box. Directly behind the circle, on the inside of the box, glue the mirror. Print SEE THE SPECIAL PERSON above the opening and decorate box.) Invite each child to peek inside and discover the Special Person.

Name Code

CHILDREN WILL

>hunt for their own name
>identify their own name
>experience success when they find their name
>experience having their name make them a winner

MATERIALS

>Mirror, 3" x 5" cards, marker

PROCEDURE

>(Teacher preparation: Print each child's name in reverse mirror image on a card. Mix up cards.) Choose a card. Hold it up to the mirror. Test the cards until your own name is found.

Sand Table

CHILDREN WILL

      print name in sand

      feel sand

      feel shape of letters of their name in sand

      experience printing in a non-threatening way (easy to fix a mistake)

      accomplish a task in a given time

      take turns

MATERIALS

      Large, low-sided box with 1" of sand; minute timer or stopwatch

PROCEDURE

      Print first name in sand. Smooth out sand when finished. Set a time of 1 or 2 minutes for each turn.

Thumbprints

CHILDREN WILL

      feel thumb on ink pad

      make thumbprint

      look at print with magnifying glass

      compare many prints

      learn that their own thumbprints are unique

MATERIALS

      Ink pad, unlined 3" x 5" cards, several magnifying glasses

PROCEDURE

      Make thumbprint on card. Study it with the magnifying glass. Compare it to other children's prints. Try to find one exactly like yours.

Crafts

Shoebox People

CHILDREN WILL

    draw self

    identify hair and eye color

    observe differences among children

MATERIALS

    Markers; glue; yarn; for each child: small shoebox without a lid, oval shaped paper, approximately same size as box

PROCEDURE

    Draw self-portrait on oval shaped paper. Stand box on end. Glue face to box. Glue appropriately colored yarn "hair" to top.

Name Banner

CHILDREN WILL

    feel felt letters

    spell own name

    glue name to banner

    read a message that says God loves them

    make something that will remind them of God's love

MATERIALS

    For each child: 7" x 10" rectangle of pinked fabric, felt block letters to spell "God Loves (*child's name*)," drinking straw, 18" of yarn, glue

PROCEDURE

    (Teacher preparation: punch 2 holes near top of banner, 2" from either end. Put straw through holes. Thread yarn through holes and tie securely. Glue "God loves" to each banner.) Glue on name. Read message. Take home. Hang in a special place.

Coat of Arms Treasure Box

CHILDREN WILL

    print name

    identify things they like

    draw things they like

    read "God loves me"

    make a personalized container for things they treasure

    see that people like different things, yet God loves everyone

MATERIALS

    Markers; white wrapping paper; for each child: 2 lb. cheese box

PROCEDURE

(Teacher preparation: Wrap top of each box securely with wrapping paper. Print GOD LOVES ME on the 2 small ends. Put tops and bottoms together. Give 1 box to each child.) Use favorite color to print name on top surface of box. Draw a pet or favorite toy on 1 side surface. Draw a favorite food on the remaining surface. Read motto on the ends of the box. Take home. Keep little "treasures" inside.

Class "My Senses" Books

CHILDREN WILL

think about their sense of sight
draw something they like to see
see pictures of things their peers like to see
contribute to a class book
"read" a book about senses
learn that our gift of sight is a gift from God

MATERIALS

1 large construction-paper eye for cover; markers; stapler; 1 eye-shaped piece of paper for each child

PROCEDURE

(Teacher preparation: Print I LIKE TO SEE at the top of eye, and THANK YOU, GOD at the bottom. Hand out eye-shaped paper and markers.) Draw something you like to see. Print name on back. Read the book after teacher has stapled all eye pages together. (Teacher: Follow same procedure for the other senses.)

Movement
Name Hunt

PROCEDURE

Decorate the room with the children's names. Put names on balloons, desks, attendance chart, bulletin board, coat racks, etc. Challenge the children to be detectives and search for their names, counting how many times they see it.

Human Letters

PROCEDURE

Position children so they have two arm lengths of space around them. Challenge them to form the letters of their first name with their bodies. Tell them they can stand, sit, or lie down.

Name Song

PROCEDURE

Children march, "follow the leader" style, singing this song. Everyone should have a turn to be leader while his (her) verse is being sung to "Frère Jacques."

Here is *(child's first name)*
Here is *(child's first name)*
God loves him (her).
God loves him (her).
We are glad to see you.
We are glad to see you.
(name, sung in three syllables)
(name, sung in three syllables)

Motion Songs

PROCEDURE

Do appropriate motions as you sing along with Hap Palmer's "Story of Sammy" or Carey Landry's "If I Were a Butterfly."

Mail Call Game

MATERIALS

Large bag for mail; for each child: a letter that says "God loves *(name)*. He (she) is special." These could be in an envelope or folded and sealed with a sticker and should be addressed to each child.

PROCEDURE

The first child pulls a letter from the mailbag. Help the child read the name. The child delivers the letter as he (she) says, "This is for *(name)*. God loves *(name)*. He (she) is special." The named child then pulls out a letter and delivers it while repeating the same message. Continue until all have had a turn. This game gives children a chance to learn each other's names, to affirm each other, and to experience being affirmed by their peers.

I Am Glad That God Made Me
(A Song with Motions)

PROCEDURE

Do appropriate motions as you sing this song (tune: "Twinkle, Twinkle Little Star"):

I am glad that God made me. *(smile; point to self)*
I am one and one only. *(hold up 1 finger; turn in place)*
I thank God for wanting me. *(fold hands in prayer)*
I thank God for loving me. *(hug self)*
I am glad that God made me. *(smile; point to self)*
I am nice, don't you agree? *(step forward; point to others)*

Prayer

Prayer Activity

MATERIALS

A small hand-mirror in a brown bag for each child

PROCEDURE

Hand each child a bag and tell each not to open it until all are ready. Explain that inside the bag is a picture of someone God loves very much. When all have a bag, ask them to look inside to discover who that person is. Ask them to look at the person in the "picture" as you lead them through this meditation:

Look in the mirror and you will see the person that God wanted you to be. Look at your eyes. God gave you eyes so you could see puppy dogs and butterflies and rainbows. Look at your ears. God gave you ears so you could hear music and jokes and someone say (*whisper*) "I love you." Wiggle your nose. God gave you a nose so you could smell roses and pizza. Look at your tongue and your teeth. God gave them to you so you could talk and share your good ideas and so you could taste cookies and milk. Look at your smile. God made you a loving person so you could make other people feel happy. God made you all and you are all wonder-full! Let's thank God by saying together, "Thank you, God, for making me so special."

RESPONSE PRAYER

PROCEDURE

Ask each child to come forward as you pray:

Teacher and all children: Thank you, God, for making (*name*).
Child who is named: Dear God, I'm glad I'm me.
(*Continue until all have been named.*)

REPEAT PRAYER

PROCEDURE

Children repeat after teacher:
Loving God,/ we are happy/ that you made us./ Help us to be/ the best we can be./ Amen.

Music

Aren't You Glad You're You? CTW 22083.
>(Children's Television Workshop, 1 Lincoln Plaza, New York, NY 10023).
>"My Name"
>"Believe in Yourself"
>"Special"
>"Me/You"

Getting to Know Myself: Hap Palmer. 10-AR 543.
>(Educational Activities, Inc., P.O. Box 392, Freeport, NY, 11520).
>"Story of Sammy"

Hi, God 2. 27262.
>(North American Liturgy Resources, 2110 W. Peoria Ave., Phoenix, AZ, 85029).
>"If I Were a Butterfly"

Mister Rogers: Won't You Be My Neighbor? MRN-8101.
>(Family Communications, 4802 Fifth Avenue, Pittsburgh, PA 15213).
>"Everybody's Fancy"
>"It's Such a Good Feeling"
>"It's You I Like"

Muppet Masquerade. CTW 161-B.
>(Children's Television Workshop, 1 Lincoln Plaza, New York, NY 10023).
>"Just One Me"
>"Aren't You Glad You're You?"
>"Wonderful Me"
>"Proud of Me"

Books

Aliki. *My Feet*. New York: Thomas Y. Crowell, 1990.

Aliki. *My Five Senses*. New York: Thomas Y. Crowell, 1962.

Anholt, Catherine and Laurence. *What I Like*. New York: G.P. Putnam's Sons, 1991.

Aylesworth, Jim. *Mary's Mirror*. New York: Holt, Rinehart & Winston, 1982.

Bach, Alice. *Warren Weasle's Worse Than Measles*. New York: Harper & Row, 1980.

Carlson, Nancy. *I Like Me*. New York: Viking Kestrel, 1988.

de Regniers, Beatrice. *Everyone Is Good for Something*. Boston: Houghton Mifflin, 1980.

Fitzhugh, Louise. *I Am Five*. New York: Delacorte Press, 1978.

Fitzhugh, Louise. *I Am Four*. New York: Delacorte Press, 1982.

Fitzhugh, Louise. *I Am Three*. New York: Delacorte Press, 1982.

Hallinan, P. K. *I'm Glad to Be Me*. Chicago: Children's Press, 1977.

Hazen, Barbara Shook. *To Be Me*. Elgin, Ill.: Child's World, 1975.

Hazen, Barbara Shook. *Very Shy*. New York: Human Sciences Press, Inc., 1982.

Kraus, Robert. *Leo, the Late Bloomer*. New York: Windmill Books, 1971.

Peet, Bill. *Pamela Camel*. Boston: Houghton Mifflin, 1984.

Sadler, Marilyn. *It's Not Easy Being a Bunny*. New York: Beginner Books, 1983.

Sharmat, Marjorie. *I'm Terrific*. New York: Holiday House, 1977.

Turnage, Shelia. *Trout the Magnificent*. San Diego: Harcourt, Brace, Jovanovich, 1984.

Tusa, Tricia. *Chicken*. New York: Macmillan, 1986.

Wold, Jo Anne. *Tell Them My Name Is Amanda*. Chicago: Whitman, 1977.

Parent Page

Ideas for doing things for or with your child and family to develop self-esteem:

Greet your child with a welcoming face and voice.

Call your child by name, lovingly.

Tell your child, "I love you."

Hug your child every day.

Show your child pictures and repeat stories from his (her) birth and baby days.

Teach your child to make a bed, hang up clothes, put away toys, get washed.

Look at your child when he (she) is talking to you.

Assign your child simple chores to help the family (set the table, take out trash, etc.) This teaches the child that he (she) is needed.

Answer your child's questions honestly.

Bless your child by making the sign of the cross on his (her) forehead at bed-time.

Surprise your child with a favorite snack.

Let your child lead you on a discovery walk. Take time to look at what your child finds.

Read to your child.

Play a game of your child's choosing.

Ask your child to teach you a song he (she) has learned.

Pray with your child. Let your child hear you thank God for him (her).

Encourage your child to try new things. Teach him (her) that it's important to keep trying when things are difficult. Applaud perseverance.

Make a "Star" board. Post accomplishments of family members.

Give your child a part in family traditions (help set the table for a special meal, prepare food, decorate the Christmas tree, etc.).

Display your child's handiwork where all can enjoy it.

"I have called you by name: You are mine." —Isaiah 43:1

CHAPTER 2

FAMILY

Discussion

TEACHER BACKGROUND

The family, as the basic unit of society and of the church, is the most important unit in our lives. It is within family that children first experience being a part of a loving group—a miniature Christian community. Children who feel love and trust within their families naturally learn to love and trust God and to extend that love and trust to others.

Your goals for a lesson about family might include teaching children that they are part of a group that offers them love, security, and care; that the family is a gift from God; and that they are an important part of their family group.

Be sensitive to those children who live with one parent and to those who live in more than one family group. Instead of saying "God loves the Jones family," you might need to say, "God loves Mary's family." Allow a child who lives in two family groups to talk about both. Assure children that although all families are different, God loves them all. The sense of security that children get from belonging to a family and knowing that they are loved and accepted teaches them what God's love is like. This gives children the necessary foundation on which they will build their future relationships with God.

QUESTIONS

Who are the people in your family?

Who in your family loves you very much?

How does their love make you feel? (Tell them that that is how God's love for them feels.)

What are some things families do together?

When do you eat with your family? have fun? work? pray?

What does someone in your family teach you to do?

What are some things you like to do with your family?

How do the people in your family help you?

What can you do to help those in your family?

Why do you think God gave you your family?

Discovery Centers
Puppet Families

CHILDREN WILL
> co-operate with others
> identify a family unit
> discover that family units can be different
> work a puppet
> role-play a family member
> practice problem solving

MATERIALS
> hand, stick, or finger puppets depicting adults and children; several situation cards

PROCEDURE
> (Teacher preparation: Print a few words on cards to suggest a family activity, i.e., picnic, wash dog, clean cellar.) Work in small groups. Choose puppets to make up a family unit. Choose a card. Use the puppets to act out the situation.

Gingerbread Families
CHILDREN WILL
> identify family members
> draw faces and decorate bodies
> see themselves as part of a unit
> see that family units are different

MATERIALS
> Cut-outs of "gingerbread"-shaped people (large for adults, medium for children, smaller for babies); crayons; optional: popsicle sticks and tape

PROCEDURE
> Take 1 cut-out for each member of your family. Draw face. Decorate body. (Optional: to make stick puppets, tape popsicle stick to back.)

Photography Studio
CHILDREN WILL
> identify family members
> compromise while choosing costumes
> dress up like family members
> take turns
> role-play family members
> interact with "photographer"
> see themselves dressed as a particular family member

MATERIALS
　　Adult and children's clothing, i.e., hats, purses, jackets, shoes, gloves, neck-
　　ties, etc.; empty 11" x 14" frame with no back *or* cardboard frame; family mem-
　　ber signs (Mother, Father, Baby, Sister, Grandfather, etc.); mirror; old camera
　　or small box to represent camera

PROCEDURE
　　Choose a sign. Dress up like that person. Go to the "photography studio." The
　　child designated as photographer "takes" the picture. To "see" the picture, the
　　child being photographed looks through the frame as the photographer holds
　　up the mirror.

Family Kitchen

CHILDREN WILL
　　prepare and serve food
　　eat a snack
　　take turns
　　role-play family members helping each other
　　share responsibilities of cleaning

MATERIALS
　　Small table and one chair; crackers; tray; plastic knife; peanut butter; napkins;
　　sponge; family name signs

PROCEDURE
　　2 children choose name signs. Role-play: 1 is hungry; the other fixes a snack.
　　(Limit snack to 1 cracker.) The child who eats throws away napkin; the child
　　who serves wipes off table. Switch places.

Crafts

Family Wreath

CHILDREN WILL

> identify family members
> draw self
> draw family members
> glue pictures of family to wreath
> see self as part of family unit
> make a wreath to share with their family

MATERIALS

> Crayons; glue sticks; masking tape; for each child: two 18" lengths of floral wire; 16 paper hearts, approximately 4" wide; 8" of ribbon

PROCEDURE

> (Teacher preparation: Attach 2 lengths of wire together at both ends to form a 10" circle for each child. Tape 8 hearts to each circle, making a wreath.) Draw yourself and everyone in your family on the hearts. Decorate the extras. Glue each heart over 1 of the taped hearts. Tie on the ribbon to make a loop for hanging.

My Home (Option 1)

CHILDREN WILL

> glue shapes to make their home
> see that different families have different kinds of homes
> see that families belong together in a special place
> make a home for their gingerbread family

MATERIALS

> Assorted paper geometric shapes; glue sticks; for each child: brown lunch bag; gingerbread families (from Discovery Centers activity)

PROCEDURE

> Glue geometric shapes to bag to make picture of your home. *(Children who live in 2 homes can make 1 on the front and 1 on the back.)* Store gingerbread family inside.

My Home (Option 2)

CHILDREN WILL

> draw their home
> see that different families have different kinds of homes
> see that families have a special place to be together
> make a folder to keep their gingerbread families in

Family Wreath

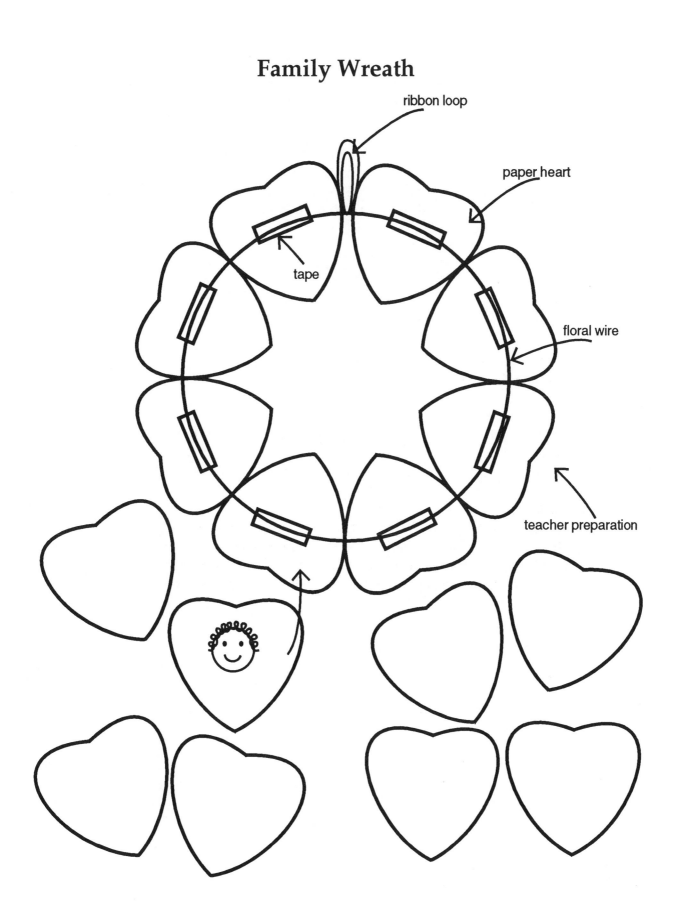

ribbon loop

paper heart

tape

floral wire

teacher preparation

MATERIALS

Crayons; glue sticks; for each child: light-colored construction paper; gingerbread families (from Discovery Centers activity)

PROCEDURE

Position construction paper with long side at bottom. Fold bottom up, making a 2" pocket. Fold paper in half, vertically. Re-open. Glue down the 2" pocket at center and at right and left edges, securing pocket. Print GOD LOVES (*child's first name*)'s FAMILY across the pocket. Draw home on cover. Insert gingerbread family in pocket.

Family Portrait

CHILDREN WILL

draw self
draw individual family members
see themselves as part of a group
glue their portait into a frame
read that God loves their family

MATERIALS

1 shirt-sized gift box for every 2 children; drawing paper to fit inside box, crayons, glue stick, sign that says "God loves (*child's first name*)'s family," 2" pieces of sponge, poster paint, aluminum pie pans

PROCEDURE

(Teacher preparation: Pour a little paint into aluminum pie pans. Give each child a sponge and one-half of a box.) Paint edges of box with sponges. While that is drying, draw yourself and all the members of your family on the drawing paper. Glue the paper into the box. Glue the sign onto the frame.

Movement

Family Stretch

PROCEDURE

Stand in a circle. Hold up the appropriate number of fingers as you do the movements suggested by this rhyme:

One and a two and a three and a four!
If you like families, touch the floor!
Five and a six and a seven and eight!
Reach up high if *your* family's great!

Let Me Tell You About My Family

PROCEDURE

Form a large circle. Hold hands, walk or skip in a circle for the opening verse. Pantomime appropriate movements in the succeeding verses. Make the song as long or short as you want, following the pattern to add verses about different family members performing loving actions (tune: "Here We Go 'Round the Mulberry Bush"):

Let me tell you about my family,
About my family, about my family,
Let me tell you about my family,
My family loves and cares for me!

This is the way Mom fixes my bike,
Fixes my bike, fixes my bike,
This is the way Mom fixes my bike,
Because she loves and cares for me!

Families Are for Loving
(Creative Dramatics)

PROCEDURE

Divide children into 2 groups: "children" and "parents." Read a situation and call on a "child" to pantomime it. The "child" will call on a "parent" to pantomime a response. The "parent" will choose a "child" to do the next situation, and so on, until everyone has had a turn.

Sample Situations:
You fell and scraped your knee.
You wanted to hear a story before bedtime.
You got lost in the park.
You colored on the living room wall with crayon.
You needed help in learning how to ride a bike.
You had a bad dream and were afraid to go back to sleep.

You played with Dad's camera after you were told not to touch it.
You came home from school after having a very bad day.
You wanted someone to play ball with you.
You needed a toy that was on a shelf too high for you to reach.

The Grandfather in the House

PROCEDURE

Form a large circle. Have children wear family member name signs: Mom, Dad, Aunt, Grandpa, etc. Ask the child wearing the "grandfather" sign to stand inside the circle. The other children hold hands and circle around the grandfather while they sing. The grandfather will choose another family member to come into the circle. That person chooses another, and so on, until the family stands together (tune: "The Farmer in the Dell"):

The Grandfather in the house!
The Grandfather in the house!
Hi-ho, away we go!
The Grandfather in the house!

The Grandfather picks the (*name a family member*)!
The Grandfather picks the (*family member*)!
Hi-ho, away we go!
The Grandfather picks the (*family member*)!

The family stands together!
The family stands together!
Hi-ho, away we go!
The family stands together!

Prayer

Prayer Activity

PROCEDURE

Mark a large circle or square on the floor with chalk or tape. Invite the children to bring their gingerbread families (from Discovery Centers activity) with them into the circle. Tell them:

"God loves us very much and doesn't want us to be alone, so God gives us families who love and help and teach and take care of us. I wonder how many people God gives us to care for us? Let's be very quiet and watchful, and we will see how many."

Ask the children, one by one, to place each of their gingerbread people on the line. Keep the children focused on the growing number, until, finally, when all the gingerbread people have been placed, you proclaim joyfully, "Look how *many* people God has given us to care for us!"

Lead the children in a cheer: "Hooray for God! Hooray for families!" *(much applause)*

Hold hands and sing a family song, such as "Let There Be Sunshine."

RESPONSE PRAYER

Teacher: Dear God, you love us.
Children: Thank you, God. *(fold hands in prayer)*
Teacher: You gave us people to care for us.
Children: Thank you, God. *(extend hands outward, palms up)*
Teacher: You gave us our families.
Children: Thank you, God. *(raise hands high in praise)*

REPEAT PRAYER

PROCEDURE

Children repeat after teacher:
Loving God,/ I love my family./ Help me to be/ a good helper/ for my family./ Amen.

Music

Backwards Land: Hap Palmer. HP-100.
>(Hap-Pal Music, Box 323, Topanga, CA 90290)
>"Helping Mommy in the Kitchen"
>"When Daddy Was a Little Boy"

Songs for the Wonder of God Series: Celebrate! 2322-8.
>(Raven Music (BMI), 4107 Woodland Park Ave. N., Seattle, WA 98103)
>"People Who Care"
>"Song for Everyone"

Hi, God! 27260
>(North American Liturgy Resources, 2110 W. Peoria Ave., Phoenix, AZ 85029)
>"What Makes Love Grow"

Peaceable Kingdom: Mary Lou Walker. JOR-7006.
>(Our Sunday Visitor, Music Publishing, Huntington, IN 46750)
>"Families Are Fun"
>"Family"
>"Child in the House"
>"Family Thank You"

10 Carrot Diamond: Songs and Stories by Charlotte Diamond. CD-317.
>(Hug Bug Records, Box 58174, Station L, Vancouver, B. C. Canada)
>"Why Did I Have to Have a Sister?"
>"May There Always Be Sunshine"

Books

Banish, Roslyn. *I Want to Tell You About My Baby*. Berkeley: Wingbow Press, 1982.

Bauer, Caroline Feller. *My Mom Travels a Lot*. New York: Frederick Warne, 1981.

Boegehold, Betty. *Daddy Doesn't Live Here Any More*. Racine, Wisc.: Western Publishing Co., 1985.

Boyd, Lizi. *The Not-So-Wicked Stepmother*. New York: Viking Kestrel, 1987.

Casely, Judith. *The Cousins*. New York: Greenwillow Books, 1990.

DePaola, Tomie. *Now One Foot, Now the Other*. New York: G.P. Putnam's Sons, 1981.

Flournoy, Valerie. *Patchwork Quilt*. New York: Dial Books, 1985.

Hallinan, P.K. *We're Very Good Friends, My Uncle and I*. Chicago: Children's Press, 1989.

Hamm, Diane Johnston. *How Many Feet in the Bed?* New York: Simon & Schuster, 1991.

Hazen, Barbara. *Even If I Did Something Awful*. New York: Atheneum, 1981.

Hines, Anna. *Daddy Makes the Best Spaghetti*. Boston: Houghton Mifflin Co., 1986.

Hines, Anna. *Grandpa Gets Grumpy*. Boston: Houghton Mifflin Co., 1988.

Lasker, Joe. *He's My Brother*. Chicago: Albert Whitman & Co., 1974

Lasky, Kathryn. *I Have Four Names for My Grandfather*. Boston: Little, Brown & Co., 1976.

Polushkin, Maria. *Baby Brother Blues*. New York: Bradbury Press, 1987.

Pryor, Bonnie. *Amanda and April*. New York: William Morrow & Co., 1986.

Seuling, Barbara. *What Kind of Family Is This?* Racine, Wisc.: Western Publilshing Co., 1985.

Titherington, Jeanne. *A Place for Ben*. New York: Greenwillow Books, 1987.

Wickstrom, Lois. *Oliver: A Story About Adoption*. Wayne, Pa.: Our Child Press, 1991.

Winthrop, Elizabeth. *Sloppy Kisses*. New York: Macmillan, 1980.

Parent Page

Ideas for doing things with your child and family to strengthen the family unit.

Share a meal together every day.

Plan a picnic for the next snowy/rainy day; eat indoors, sitting around on a blanket on the floor.

Take a walk; take turns praising God for the beauty you see.

Bake cookies together.

Get a picture book from the library. Let each person "read" a page.

Play "Laundry Co." Sort clean laundry, fold, deliver to owner.

Tell jokes!

Finish the sentence, "When I was a baby…"

Work together to help a neighbor.

Go to church together. Afterwards, share breakfast with another family.

Write a family letter to a relative, with each family member writing or drawing a message.

Give each person a special job to do to help the family. Once a week at a family meal thank each other for the specific ways each has helped.

Make and/or look at a family snapshot album.

Tell your child the story of his (her) birth.

At bedtime, pray together, thanking God for things that happened that day.

Help each other with chores.

Tell your child the story of your courtship and wedding.

Make a poster or bulletin board showing relative's pictures.

Have a "game night." Each week, let a different person choose a game that all can play.

Have a family picture taken. Display it in a prominent position in your home.

"You are the bows from which your children as living arrows are sent forth."
—Kahlil Gibran

CHAPTER 3

FRIENDS

Discussion

BACKGROUND

Friendship is a basic human need, as necessary to total health as food and shelter. It produces feelings of acceptance and security, important ingredients in the formation of a positive self-image. Experiencing the warmth of friendship enables us to understand the depth of Jesus' love when he says, "I am your friend."

Children learn about friendship by experiencing it. The care, love, and help that parents give their children teach them the basics of friendship. This is the necessary first step in the life-long process of learning how to make friends and how to be a good friend.

Teachers join parents in nurturing this process by modeling friendly behavior and by providing opportunities for children to practice it. Children are great imitators. When they see adults welcoming, listening, taking turns, and helping, they will try to do the same. When they are the recipients of this behavior, they will like the feeling that comes with it and they'll recognize friendship as something desirable. They'll be open to learning how to make these nice feelings last. Adults can help children learn to be friendly by encouraging them to take turns, share, listen to one another, and help one another and by teaching them the words to use to communicate with respect.

QUESTIONS

Who is your friend? How do you know that?

What do friends do together?

What do you like about friends?

How does it make you feel when a friend lets you play with one of his (her) toys?

What are some things a friend has helped you with?

Are you a good friend to someone? How do you show you are a good friend?

What would you do if you had a snack and your friend didn't?

What would you do if there was a special toy that you and your friend both wanted to play with?

Discovery Centers

Puzzle Hearts

CHILDREN WILL

    pick up puzzle pieces

    sort colors (young children)

    co-operate

    put puzzle pieces together

    build a sentence about friendship

    read (or hear) a message about friendship

MATERIALS

    6 paper hearts with friendship messages printed on them, e.g., "Jesus is my friend," "Friends take turns," "Friends share," etc.

PROCEDURE

    (Teacher preparation: Cut hearts into 2 or 3 pieces and mix up all the pieces. Note: For very young children, use different colored paper for each heart. For older children, use all the same color.) Find a partner and work together to form hearts from the pieces. Read, or ask the teacher to read, the messages. Mix up the pieces so others can have a turn to make the puzzles.

Phone-a-Friend

CHILDREN WILL

    decide whom to call

    phone someone

    talk to someone on the phone

    extend friendship

    practice friendly behavior

MATERIALS

    Toy telephones or paper-cup phones. (Punch a hole in the bottom of 2 cups. Insert 1 end of a 72" piece of string or yarn in each. Knot ends.)

PROCEDURE

    Call a friend in class. Have a conversation. Take turns calling and answering.

Friends' Railroad

CHILDREN WILL

    use imaginations

    co-operate

    set up a railroad

    take turns being engineer, ticket agent, ticket taker, passengers

    wear hats and name signs

    play together

MATERIALS

3 or 4 cardboard boxes, large enough for children to sit in. (Label 1 of them "Friends' Railroad Engine"); assortment of hats; paper tickets; name signs for engineer, ticket agent, ticket taker, passengers

PROCEDURE

Set up train. Choose a name sign and corresponding hat. Sell and buy tickets, board train, collect tickets, go for a ride. Let other children play, or switch positions.

Friend Bookmark

CHILDREN WILL

use stamp pad and rubber stamps
color stamped images
make a gift
identify a friend
give a gift

MATERIALS

Rectangles (2 1/2" x 7") of colored card-stock paper with BE MY FRIEND printed on 1 side; ink pads; rubber stamps; markers or colored pencils

PROCEDURE

Decorate the bookmark using rubber stamps and colored pencils or markers. Give to a friend.

Crafts

My Friends Autograph Book

CHILDREN WILL

> line up holes in paper
> secure brads
> assemble a booklet
> choose, arrange, and glue pictures and a title to the cover
> ask friends to print their name or draw a picture
> sign or draw in someone else's book
> see that they have many friends

MATERIALS

> Markers; glue; pre-cut pictures from greeting cards or gift catalogues; for each child: 6 sheets of wide-lined paper; 2 sheets of construction paper that is 1" longer and wider than the lined paper; 2 brads; one 4" x 3" sign with MY FRIENDS printed on it

PROCEDURE

> (Teacher preparation: Punch 2 holes in all the paper so it can be put together, booklet style.) Line up the holes in all the paper, placing the construction paper on the top and bottom of the pile. Put brads through the holes. Glue "My Friends" and pre-cut pictures to the cover. Collect friends' names or drawings in your book.

Friendship "Video"

CHILDREN WILL

> draw a picture of something they like to do with a friend
> narrate the drawing during the class "video" show
> take turns talking and listening
> hear and see how others have fun with friends

MATERIALS

> Large cardboard box, at least 20" x 16"; 2 dowels, 6" longer than the height of the box; roll of butcher paper, tape, crayons

PROCEDURE

> (Teacher preparation: Cut a 15" x 12" opening in the front of the box to make the "screen." Cut 2 holes in the top and 2 in the bottom at each side of the screen. Insert the dowels. Decorate box to look like TV set. Tape butcher paper to the chalkboard or wall. Mark off 15" x 12" rectangle for each child, spacing rectangles 18" apart.) Draw a pictue inside the rectangle of something you like to do with a friend. After all are finished, the teacher will tape 1 end of the paper to a dowel. Roll tightly. Tape the other end of the paper to the other dowel. Turn the dowels. As each picture appears on the screen, the child who drew it will come up and tell the others about it.

Sand/Sun Picture

CHILDREN WILL

    draw on sandpaper

    print a friend's name and own name

    glue on a friendship sentence

    look at the picture with sunshine or light behind it

    read or hear why friends are like sunshine

    give a gift

MATERIALS

    Crayons; iron; newspaper; glue; for each child: 5" square piece of medium sandpaper; 1 piece of colored typing paper with a 5" square drawn in center; sign that says "Friends are like sunshine. They make us feel bright and cheerful."

PROCEDURE

    (Teacher preparation: Print TO and FROM in the bottom border.) Pressing hard with crayons, draw a simple picture on the rough side of the sandpaper. Take turns taking sandpaper picture and colored typing paper to teacher. Center sandpaper, picture side down, in the frame on the typing paper. Teacher will press with a warm iron. (Note: place newspaper underneath typing paper.) Glue friendship sentence to top border. Fill in the "To" and "From." Hold up to the sun to see the picture "light up." Give to a friend.

Movement

Be My Friend Hand Clap
PROCEDURE

Choose a partner and face each other. Clap hands to this verse:

Friends are kind; *(hit hands on own thighs, together, on partner's hands)*
Friends are nice. *(hit hands on own thighs, together, on partner's hands)*
Be my friend; now don't think twice. *(hit hands on own thighs, together, right to right, together, left to left, together, on partner's hands)*
We'll have fun *(hit hands on own thighs, together, on partner's hands)*
Every day. *(hit hands on own thighs, together, on partner's hands)*
Come on, now, what do you say? *(hit hands on own thighs, together, right to right, together, left to left, together, on partner's hands)*

Come and Play Circle Game
PROCEDURE

Sit in a circle. 1 child walks around the outside of the circle, touching each child on the shoulder as everyone sings (tune: "Row, Row, Row Your Boat"):

Friend, friend, come and play,/come and play with me;
Running, skipping, hopping, jumping,/ happy we will be!

The person who is touched on the word "me" enters the circle with the person who was "it." They hop, jump, skip, clap hands, or do any other motion they choose while the rest of the children sing the last two lines. The friend becomes "it" and the game continues. Play until everyone has had a turn to be in the circle.

Find a Friend Mix-Up
MATERIALS

Enough paper hearts that say "Be my friend," for one-half the class.

PROCEDURE

(Teacher preparation: Cut the hearts in half using a zig-zag or scallop cut so that no 2 are cut alike.) Mix up the halves and give 1 to each child. Tell the children to move around the room, trying to find the friend who is holding the half that will complete theirs. When 2 pieces match, the 2 friends should sit together and ask each other a personal question, i.e., "What is your favorite food?" When all are ready, let each child introduce his (her) friend by saying, "This is my friend *(name)* and his (her) favorite food is *(name food)*."

Mountain of Friendship
MATERIALS

10 coffee cans; wrapping paper with hearts drawn on it; twenty 3" x 5" cards with assorted friendly and unfriendly traits printed on them

PROCEDURE

(Teacher preparation: Cover coffee cans.) Spread cards out, face down. The first child chooses a card. Read the card out loud. Decide if it is a friendly or unfriendly trait. If it is a friendly trait, add a can to the mountain. If it is an unfriendly trait, subtract a can. (Build the mountain pyramid style, with 4 cans making up the bottom row, then 3, then 2, then 1.) The next child chooses a card and proceeds in the same way. When the mountain is completed, start a new game.

F-r-i-e-n-d

PROCEDURE

Make a large circle. Face 1 direction and skip to the first 2 lines of the following chant. Find a partner and swing arm in arm on the last two lines.

F-R-I-E-N-D!
I hope you'll be a friend to me!
I'll like you and you'll like me!
We'll have fun; just wait and see!

Prayer

Prayer Activity

PROCEDURE

Form a circle and hold hands. Raise arms up high each time you sing, "Praise him!"

Teacher:

Jesus is our very good friend. He listens when we talk to him. He helps us. He loves us and cares for us. Let's sing this song to show we are happy that he is our friend.

My best friend is Jesus. Praise him! Praise him!
My best friend is Jesus. Praise him!

Jesus loves me truly. Praise him! Praise him!
Jesus loves me truly. Praise him!

RESPONSE PRAYER

Teacher: Loving God, I want to be a good friend. Friends listen.
Children: Help me to listen.
Teacher: Friends care.
Children: Help me to care.
Teacher: Friends help.
Children: Help me to help.
Teacher: Friends share.
Children: Help me to share.

REPEAT PRAYER

PROCEDURE

Children repeat after teacher:
Loving God,/we are glad/ you gave us friends./ Help me to be/ a good friend, too./ Amen.

My Best Friend Is Jesus

1. My best friend is Je - sus.   Praise   him!   Praise   him!
2. Je - sus loves me tru - ly.   Praise   him!   Praise   him!

1. My best friend is Je - sus.   Pra - ise   him!
2. Je - sus loves me tru - ly.   Pra - ise   him!

Music

Bob's Favorite Street Songs. 7502104144.
>   (A & M Records, Inc., P.O. Box 118, Hollywood, CA 90078).
>   "Hi, Friend!"
>   "Somebody Come and Play"

Bullfrogs and Butterflies. BWR 2010.
>   (Sparrow Records, Inc., 8587 Canoga Ave., Canoga Park, CA 91304).
>   "Friends"
>   "You're So Good to Me"

Getting to Know Myself: Hap Palmer. 10-AR-543.
>   (Educational Activities, Inc., Box 392, Freeport, NY 11520).
>   "Won't You Be My Friend?"

Mr. Rogers: Won't You Be My Neighbor? MRN-8101.
>   (Family Communications, 4802 Fifth Ave., Pittsburgh, PA 15213).
>   "Won't You Be My Neighbor?"

Uncle Ruthie: Take a Little Step. UR-01.
>   (Uncle Ruthie Buel, 1731 S. Sherbourne Dr., Los Angeles, CA 90035).
>   "The Person Next to You"
>   "The Very Song"

Books

Anglund, Joan Walsh. *A Friend is Someone Who Likes You*. New York: Harcourt, Brace & World, 1958.

Crary, Elizabeth. *I Want to Play*. Seattle: Parenting Press, 1982.

Delton, Judy. *Lee Henry's Best Friend*. Chicago: Albert Whitman & Co., 1980.
Delton, Judy. *The New Girl at School*. New York: E.P. Dutton, 1979.
Delton, Judy. *Two Is Company*. New York: Crown Publishers, 1976.

Hickman, Martha. *My Friend William Moved Away*. Nashville: Abingdon Press, 1979.

King, Larry. *Because of Lozo Brown*. New York: Viking Kestrel, 1988.
Kubler, Susanne. *The Three Friends*. New York: Macmillan, 1984.

Majewski, Joe. *A Friend for Oscar Mouse*. New York: Dial Books, 1988.
Minarik, Elsa. *Little Bear's Friend*. New York: Harper, 1960.

Numeroff, Laura. *Amy for Short*. New York: Macmillan, 1976.

Raynor, Dorka. *My Friends Live in Many Places*. Chicago: Albert Whitman & Co., 1980.
Rogers, Fred. *Making Friends*. New York: G.P. Putnam's Sons, 1987.

Schumacher, Claire. *Tim and Jim*. New York: Dodd, Mead & Co., 1987.

Varley, Susan. *Badger's Parting Gifts*. New York: Lothrop, Lee & Shepard, 1984.

Wade, Anne. *A Promise Is for Keeping*. Chicago: Children's Press, 1979.
Weiss, Nicki. *Maude and Sally*. New York: Greenwillow Books, 1983.
Wildsmith, Brian. *Lazy Bear*. New York: Watts, 1974.
Winthrop, Elizabeth. *Katherine's Doll*. New York: E.P. Dutton, 1983.

Parent Page

Ideas for doing things for and with your child and family to develop friendliness:

Wait your turn with patience—at a traffic light, stop sign, checkout counter, etc.

Praise your child for sharing and helping.

Thank a friend for helping you.

Ask your child about his (her) friends at school.

Look at your child and listen when he (she) is telling you something. Expect your child not to interrupt when you are talking.

Greet your neighbors with a friendly smile.

Take the time to help a friend. Let your child know what you're doing and why.

Provide materials for your child to make an invitation, asking a friend to visit.

Let your child accept an invitation to a friend's house.

Bake bread with your child. Together, deliver some to a friend.

Go to the playground. Take turns on the equipment.

Always say "please" and "thank you."

Be honest with your child.

Plan and go on an outing with friends.

Teach friends to share picking up toys when playtime is over.

Speak kindly about others.

Let family members take turns deciding what to have for Sunday breakfast. Insist that everyone taste the food without complaining.

Give a warm welcome to friends who visit you.

Welcome your child's friends. Learn their names.

Play your friend's favorite game.

Show respect to those who don't agree with you.

"Take the time to love; no one can love in a hurry."
— Bishop Fulton J. Sheen

CHAPTER 4

FEELINGS

Discussion

BACKGROUND

Our feelings help to make us each the unique person God created us to be. Because feelings can be powerful and complicated and sometimes seem to have a mind of their own, children can feel overpowered and frightened by their own feelings. They need caring adults to show them how to deal with their feelings. Children need to know that it's normal to have many different feelings, it's all right to express feelings, and feelings can change. They need to be assured that they can change negative feelings to positive ones, and God always loves them, no matter how they feel.

Children gain the security to explore and handle their feelings when adults listen to them, give them unconditional love, teach them to identify their feelings, and show them how to turn negative feelings around. As they learn about their own feelings, they can be encouraged to recognize the feelings of others and to develop sympathy and empathy. They'll discover that they can reach out and positively affect others' feelings.

It's important to show children that they are loved just as much when they are sad or angry as they are when they are happy so that they will come to understand that God loves them unconditionally and always.

QUESTIONS

How would you feel if someone gave you a new toy?

What would you say and do to show you were happy?

How would you feel if you lost your favorite toy?

What would you say and do to show you were sad?

Do we feel the same way all of the time?

When you are feeling sad, who can you tell? What do they do to make you feel happy?

How can you tell if your parents or friends are happy or sad? If they are sad, what can you do to make them feel happy?

Does God love you more if you are happy or if you are sad?

Discovery Centers

Clay Faces

CHILDREN WILL

feel clay

form a clay frown and smile

change the frown to a smile and the smile to a frown

identify happy and sad faces

see the faces change

MATERIALS

paper plates, clay, happy and sad signs

PROCEDURE

Form eyes, a nose, and a frown from clay. Arrange on the paper plate to make a sad face. Label it. Change the frown to a smile. Label it.

Sandpaper Mouths

CHILDREN WILL

feel sandpaper shape of smile and frown

trace smile and frown shape with their finger

make a smile and frown rubbing

trace their rubbing with their finger

name a smile and a frown

MATERIALS

Shallow box, at least 8" x 6"; sandpaper arc, approximately 1" wide and 4" long; glue; crayons with paper wrapping peeled off; paper, the same size as the box

PROCEDURE

(Teacher preparation: Glue arc into center of box. Cut paper to fit into box.) Hold box so arc looks like a smile. Trace it with your finger, feeling the roughness of the sandpaper. Turn box so the arc looks like a frown. Trace it with your finger. Place paper in the box. Rub crayon over sandpaper, making a smile. Trace the smile rubbing with your finger. Tell what it is. Make a frown rubbing. Trace over it with your finger. Tell what it is.

Show Your Feelings

CHILDREN WILL

make faces expressing different feelings

look at these different faces in a mirror

match feelings and faces

learn there are many different feelings

see that feelings and faces can change

MATERIALS
Brown lunch bag containing a small hand-mirror and 4 "feeling cards."

PROCEDURE
(Teacher preparation: Print HAPPY, SAD, ANGRY, FRIGHTENED on the cards.) Take the mirror out of bag. Choose a card. Look in the mirror and make a face that expresses the feeling on the card.

Happy/Sad Caps

CHILDREN WILL
wear a cap that shows how they feel
think of a way to make someone feel better
role-play
practice ways to change feelings
learn they have the power to change someone's feelings
be affirmed for their positive action

MATERIALS
1 cap with a happy face; 1 cap with a sad face; sad situation cards, i.e., toys are lost, friend won't play, fell down, etc.

PROCEDURE
Work in pairs. 1 child puts on a sad cap and chooses a situation card. Both read the card. The child without a cap acts out a way for the sad child to feel happy again. The sad child then wears the happy cap and thanks the friend who helped. Reverse roles.

Crafts

Wheel of Feelings

CHILDREN WILL

    color sections of wheel
    glue on feelings signs
    attach pointer with brad
    tape on paper clip
    identify own feelings
    communicate own feelings to others

MATERIALS

    For each child: 8" diameter posterboard circle, divided into 6 sections; set of 6 feelings labels, i.e., happy, sad, angry, frightened, excited, surprised; 1 brad; pre-cut paper pointer, 3" long; crayons; glue; tape

PROCEDURE

    Color each section of the circle. Glue a label in each section. Attach pointer by securing with brad at center of circle. Open the paper clip slightly and tape to the back to make a hanger. Take home and hang in a place where you can reach it. Point to your feelings each day.

Cheer-Up Rebus Cards

CHILDREN WILL

    use their imaginations
    substitute symbols or pictures for words
    draw, glue, and color to make a card
    give the card to someone who needs cheering up
    learn they can change another person's sad feelings to happy ones

MATERIALS

    Colored paper; small pre-cut pictures; markers; glue

PROCEDURE

    (Teacher preparation: Print cheer-up phrases on the chalk board. Show how to turn one into a rebus sentence. For instance, the message, "Be happy! It's a beautiful day!" could be translated into "(picture of a bee) (picture of a smile face)! It's a (picture of a bee) - U - T - ful day!" As the class thinks of ways to turn other phrases into rebus sentences, print their ideas on the board.) Copy the message you want on your card, drawing or gluing pre-cut pictures to complete it. Give it to someone who needs cheering up.

Happy/Sad Class Books

CHILDREN WILL

      draw things that make them happy or sad

      contribute their drawings to a class book

      read the class book

      see what makes their peers happy and sad

MATERIALS

      Crayons; 4 brads; 2 construction paper covers, 1 titled "My Happy Book," the other titled "My Sad Book"; for each child: 2 pieces of light colored construction paper with THIS MAKES ME HAPPY printed on 1 side, and THIS MAKES ME SAD on the other.

PROCEDURE

      Draw what makes you happy and sad. Print your name on both sheets of paper. Give to the teacher who will put the books together with brads. Take turns reading the books.

Paper Cup Puppets

CHILDREN WILL

      draw happy and sad faces

      make a puppet

      identify their own feelings

      role-play with puppet

MATERIALS

      Yarn; crayons; glue; for each child: white paper cup; toilet paper roll

PROCEDURE

      Hold cup upside down and draw a happy face on 1 side of the cup and a sad face on the other. Glue yarn hair to the top. Color toilet paper roll. Stand the cup on the toilet paper roll body. Place 2 fingers in the roll. Jiggle to turn the head.

Movement

Am I Happy? Am I Sad?

MATERIALS

Paper cup puppets (from Crafts section)

PROCEDURE

Stand and hold paper cup puppets. The teacher will name a situation ("You fell off your bike," "Mom baked your favorite cookies," "Your friend shared with you," "You were sick," etc.) After each situation that makes you feel happy, show the happy side of your puppet to the teacher. After each situation that makes you feel sad, show the sad side.

Feelings Echo Pantomime

PROCEDURE

The teacher will say a line and do a motion. The students will echo both the line and the motion.

I can feel happy. *(laugh)*
I can feel sad. *(cry)*
I can feel friendly. *(shake hands with the person on your right)*
I can feel mad. *(growl. Stomp your feet. Show your fist)*
Feelings are different *(hold hands up, quizzically)*
As "A" to "Z"; *(form letters A and Z with fingers)*
But feelings are all *(extend hands, encompassing a large space)*
A part of me! *(point 2 thumbs at self)*
Thank you, God, for my feelings! *(clap)*

Sad Sack/Jumping Jack
(A very active game)

PROCEDURE

Sit in a large circle with a frown on your face. The teacher will describe a happy or sad situation. When a happy situation is described, jump up, smile, and do jumping jacks for five seconds. When time is called, sit down and be a sad sack until another happy situation is described.

Feelings Game

MATERIALS

1 happy/sad die

PROCEDURE

(Teacher preparation: Make the happy/sad die by cutting a quart milk or juice container and folding it so it is a square. Tape securely and cover with light colored paper. Draw or glue a happy face on 3 sides and a sad face on 3 sides.) Roll the die. If a sad face appears, tell what would make you feel sad. If a happy face appears, tell what would make you happy. Give everyone a turn. (Optional: After each example of a sad situation, ask, "How could you change this sad situation to a happy one?" The child who stated the example calls on someone to answer. Give a cheer for the person who suggests a way to change the sad feelings.)

Improvisations

PROCEDURE

Spread out so that everyone has plenty of room to move. Tell the children to listen while you tell them a story. They must decide how the main character is feeling. Then they will pretend to be the main character and act out the feeling. (Make the main character an animal, plant, or element. Describe a different feeling in each story.)

Sample Stories:
It is a beautiful, sunshiny day. You are a butterfly, feeling the soft wind, smelling the flowers, drinking the nectar.

It is a cold, rainy day. You are a little kitten, far from home, trying to find your way back.

You are the wind. Something has wakened you from a deep sleep. You didn't want to be wakened.

Prayer

Prayer Activity

PROCEDURE

Form a circle. As you sing the following song (tune: "If You're Happy and You Know It") walk in one direction. On the words, "God loves me," stop and clap three times. Reverse direction on the next verse.

When I'm feeling sad and lonely, God loves me.
When I'm feeling sad and lonely, God loves me.
When I'm feeling sad and lonely, I know God is thinking of me,
When I'm feeling sad and lonely, God loves me.

When I'm feeling glad and friendly, God loves me.
(Follow same pattern as verse 1.)

RESPONSE PRAYER

Teacher: When I feel happy,
Children: you love me, God.
Teacher: When I feel sad,
Children: you love me, God.
Teacher: When I feel friendly,
Children: you love me, God.
Teacher: When I feel mad,
Children: you love me, God.
All: Thank you, God, for loving me all the time.

REPEAT PRAYER

PROCEDURE

Children repeat after teacher:
Loving God,/ you want everyone/ to be happy./ Help us/ to make others/ feel happy./ Amen.

Music

Follow That Bird. CBK1-5475.
>   (RCA Records, 1133 Avenue of the Americas, New York, NY 10036).
>   "I'm So Blue"

The Gang's All Here. CTW 22102
>   (Children's Television Workshop, 1 Lincoln Plaza, New York, NY 10023).
>   "I'm Sad Because I'm Happy"

Getting To Know Myself: Hap Palmer. 10-AR 543
>   (Educational Activities, Inc., Box 392, Freeport, NY 11520).
>   "Feeling Angry"
>   "Let Me Show You"

Hi, God! 27260.
>   (North American Liturgy Resources, 2110 W. Peoria Ave., Phoenix, AZ 85029).
>   "I Like God's Love"

Welcome! CTW 22091.
>   (Children's Television Workshop, 1 Lincoln Plaza, New York, NY 10023).
>   "Show Me How You Feel"

Books

Aliki. *Feelings*. New York: Mulberry Books, 1986.
Ancona, George. *I Feel*. New York: E.P. Dutton, 1977.

Berger, Terry. *I Have Feelings*. New York: Behavioral Publications, 1971.
Berger, Terry. *I Have Feelings, Too*. New York: Human Sciences Press, 1977.

Cohen, Miriam. *Jim's Dog Muffin*. New York: Greenwillow Books, 1984.
Conta, Marcia. *Feelings Between Kids and Grown Ups*. Milwaukee: Raintree Editions, 1974.

Keller, Holly. *Lizzie's Invitation*. New York: Greenwillow Books, 1987.
Keller, Holly. *Too Big*. New York: Greenwillow Books, 1983.
Knox-Wagner, Elaine. *My Grandpa Retired Today*. Niles, Ill.: Albert Whitman & Co., 1982.

Mayer, Mercer. *I Was So Mad*. Racine, Wisc.: Western Publishing Co., 1983.

O'Donnell, Elizabeth. *Maggie Doesn't Want to Move*. New York: Four Winds Press, 1987.

Polushkin, Maria. *Baby Brother Blues*. New York: Bradbury Press, 1987.

Rogers, Fred. *Moving*. New York: G.P. Putnam's Sons, 1987.

Scott, Ann. *Sam*. New York: McGraw Hill, 1967.
Sharmat, Marjorie. *Attila the Angry*. New York: Holiday House, 1985.
Sharmat, Marjorie. *I Want Mama*. New York: Harper & Row, 1974.
Simon, Norma. *I Am Not a Crybaby*. Niles, Ill.: Albert Whitman & Co., 1989.
Skurzynski, Gloria. *Martin by Himself*. New York: Houghton Mifflin Co., 1979.
Strauss, Joyce. *How Does It Feel?* New York: Human Sciences Press, 1981.

Yashima, Tara. *Crow Boy*. New York: Viking Press, 1955.

Parent Page

Ideas for doing things for and with your child and family to promote an understanding of feelings:

Learn a joke. Tell it to someone who looks sad.

Watch a TV program together. Talk about how it made you feel.

Remind your child to say "Thank you" to his (her) teacher. Ask how that made the teacher feel.

At bedtime, tell God about the feelings you had today. Thank him for loving you always.

Sing a song when you feel sad.

Teach your child to use "I" messages. Say, "I feel ( )." "I like/don't like ( )."

Put down your work and listen when your child wants to tell you how he/she feels.

Read a book together. Share your feelings about it.

Make a feelings chart so all in the family can show how they feel. Hang it in the kitchen.

Put a happy note in your child's lunch box.

Praise your child for making someone feel happy.

Pray for a sad friend.

Visit or call someone who is sad.

Say "I love you" to everyone in your family.

Have each family member tell 5 things that make him (her) happy and sad.

Give a hug to a sad person.

Tell your child how you feel.

Make a special "making up" snack to celebrate forgiveness.

Encourage friends who are arguing to talk about how they feel and say what would make them feel better.

Recall a time when your child was sad. Talk about what made him (her) happy again.

"The way to happiness is to make others so." — Robert Ingersoll

CHAPTER 5

SHARING

Discussion

BACKGROUND

From the beginning of Hebrew history, we see Yahweh admonishing the people to share with the less fortunate, the widows, the orphans, the foreigners. Jesus continues and expands this teaching by telling his followers to share even with their enemies. For it is by giving, he says, that we receive.

Sharing, however, can be difficult, especially for young children. Children who won't share their own chair or a favorite toy are not necessarily being selfish. Sometimes children, who are just beginning to develop a sense of self, consider their special things to be a part of them. Some might feel that having to share a favorite object is like giving up a part of themselves. Never forcing a child to share special things gives that child a sense of security. This frees the child to learn about sharing on a much larger scale.

We adults teach children to share by sharing with them, noting how happy that makes them feel, and showing how much pleasure sharing gives us. Provide opportunities for children to share supplies, snacks, toys, books, work, fun, and prayer. Encourage parents to let children share responsibilities at home. Teach children that sharing is another way to show love.

QUESTIONS

What are some things people share with you?

How do you feel when someone shares with you?

What do you say to someone who shares with you?

What do you share with others? How do your friends feel when you share with them?

How do you know how they feel?

What are some things you don't like to share? Why?

What jobs do you share with someone?

If you had a friend who had no lunch, what would you share?

If you had a friend who was feeling sad, what would you share?

Discovery Centers

Building Buddies

CHILDREN WILL

    handle building pieces
    discover that it's necessary to share
    use imagination
    share materials
    share ideas
    build something

MATERIALS

    Tinker Toys; brown paper lunch bag for each child

PROCEDURE

    (Teacher preparation: Put several uniform pieces of Tinker Toys in each bag, i.e., all rods, all spheres, all wheels, etc.) Choose a bag. Build a free-standing object. (Children will discover they can't accomplish the task alone.) Share materials with someone. Build something.

Sharing Boxes

CHILDREN WILL

    co-operate in pairing objects to make them complete
    share what they "own" with another person
    learn that sharing benefits both parties

MATERIALS

    2 boxes. Box 1 contains objects that need to be shared with things in box 2. (Example: Box 1: cassette tape player, fruit box drink, can of fruit, checkerboard. Box 2: cassette tape, straw, can opener, checkers.)

PROCEDURE

    Work in pairs. Each child "owns" 1 box. Share objects to make them complete and usable.

Book Nook

CHILDREN WILL

    co-operate in choosing a book to read
    share a book
    take turns reading
    take turns listening

MATERIALS

    Picture books about sharing; 2 small chairs

PROCEDURE

Work in pairs. Choose a book. Sit on the chairs. Take turns "reading" and listening to the story.

Puzzle Pieces

CHILDREN WILL

match colored puzzle pieces
share pieces of a puzzle
share a task
co-operate to complete a puzzle

MATERIALS

3 or 4 large-piece children's puzzles (or make your own by mounting pictures on poster board, covering with clear contact and cutting into puzzle pieces); brown lunch bag for each child

PROCEDURE

(Teacher preparation: Color code backs of puzzles. Place several pieces from 1 puzzle only in each bag. Divide puzzles so that 3 or 4 children will work on one.) Choose a bag. Find other people who have pieces from the same puzzle. Share your pieces and complete the puzzle.

Funny Face

CHILDREN WILL

share chalk
share ideas
co-operate in drawing a face

MATERIALS

Chalkboard; 1 piece of chalk

PROCEDURE

(Teacher preparation: Draw a large oval on the board.) Take turns adding 1 feature to the face.

Crafts
Create-a-Thing

CHILDREN WILL

    share ideas

    share materials

    arrange, glue, stack, or connect materials

    work together to create something

    share their creation with the class

MATERIALS

    Construction paper; glue; scissors; craft supplies: yarn, paper geometric shapes, foil, cotton balls, fabric pieces, sandpaper, toilet paper rolls, felt, pipe cleaners, drinking straws, etc.; for each child: paper lunch bag

PROCEDURE

    (Teacher preparation: Put 6 different craft items in each bag.) Work in pairs. Share the contents of your bag to create something. Everything in both bags must be used. Creations may be free-standing or glued to construction paper. Tell the class about your creation.

Magic Colors

CHILDREN WILL

    paint

    share paper

    mix their paint with their partner's

    make a new color

    co-operate to make a poster about sharing

MATERIALS

    For each 2 children: 1 large piece of water color paper; 2 brushes; 2 colors of paint: red and yellow, yellow and blue, or blue and red; 1 cup of water

PROCEDURE

    (Teacher preparation: Draw a large happy face in the upper right, upper left, and lower center of the paper. In the upper center, print FRIENDS SHARE!) Work in pairs. Each child takes 1 color and paints a face in the upper right or left. Print your name under the face you painted. Both paint the face in the lower center, creating a new color as the individual colors mix. Display for all to see.

Celebration Bread

CHILDREN WILL

    knead and shape dough

    share preparing one loaf

    smell bread baking

    wait for bread to be finished

    share the bread

Magic Colors

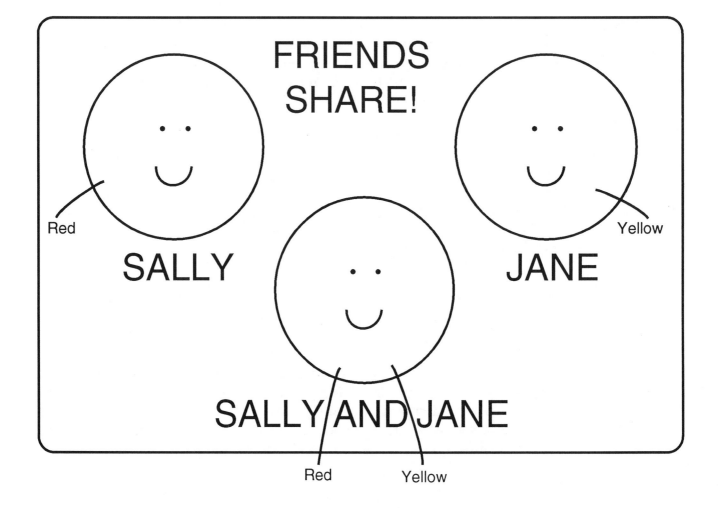

FRIENDS SHARE!

Red

SALLY

Yellow

JANE

SALLY AND JANE

Red   Yellow

MATERIALS

Frozen bread dough (thawed); margarine; heart-shaped baking pan; toaster oven

PROCEDURE

(Teacher preparation: Coat pan with margarine. Cut a plum-sized piece of dough for each child.) Knead your piece of dough. Divide it in half and shape into 2 balls. Put dough balls in pan around outer perimeter. Cover and let raise $1/2$ hour. Bake at 350 degrees for 12-15 minutes, or until golden brown. Rub margarine over top. Use in prayer activity.

Mutual Mural

CHILDREN WILL

draw a picture of something they share
share crayons
share ideas
co-operate to make a mural

MATERIALS

Long table covered with butcher paper; 1 crayon for each child

PROCEDURE

Stand around table far enough apart to have a space to draw in. Take 1 crayon. Draw a picture of something you can share. If you need another color, share with someone. When everyone is finished, hang the mural.

Movement

Shared Space Race

PROCEDURE

Divide group into pairs. Partners face each other, hold hands, extend arms straight out in front of them. The space created inside their joined arms is their shared space and must be carried over the finish line before the next pair can run. If hands are dropped, the pair must start over. Encourage everyone to cheer for the running pair. Set a time limit for the race. The whole class shares the winner's circle if all cross the finish line before time is called.

Go This Way
(A circle follow-the-leader game)

PROCEDURE

Form a circle. Each child gets a turn to enter the circle and lead the others in doing a motion as all sing (tune: "Did You Ever See a Lassie?"):

Did you ever see a *(child's name)* go this way and that way,
Go this way and that way,
Did you ever see a *(child's name)* go this way and that?

Jack-in-the-Box Chant

PROCEDURE

Form two lines, facing each other. Line one is standing; line two is squatting. Alternate standing and squatting on each line of the following chant, so that when line one squats, line two stands, and so on.

You share with me;
I share with you.
We'll share at play,
And work time, too!
We'll share a snack;
We'll share a toy;
We'll share our fun;
We'll share our joy!

Wallpaper Match-up

MATERIALS

1 piece of wallpaper, at least 6" x 8", for half the children; a stopwatch or clock with a second hand.

PROCEDURE

(Teacher preparation: Cut each piece of wallpaper into 2 pieces, puzzle style. Mix up the pieces. Give 1 piece to each child. Designate an area as the "sharing center.") Search for a person who is holding the piece of wallpaper that will match yours. When you find that person, sit together in the sharing center. To make the game more exciting, set a time limit. Everyone who reaches the sharing center within the time limit is a winner.

Shadows

MATERIALS

Audio cassette tape: "Somebody Come and Play" *(Bob's Favorite Street Songs)*

PROCEDURE

Divide the class into pairs. Spread out so that all have plenty of room to stretch. Decide who will be the "person" and who will be the "shadow." The "shadow" stands behind the "person" and will copy everything the "person" does. The "person" may *not* move his (her) feet, but may move head, arms, body. Play "Somebody Come and Play" and have the "person" move to the music and the "shadow" copy the movements. After a minute, reverse roles. Switch partners. Play again!

Prayer

Prayer Activity

MATERIALS

Heart-shaped bread from Crafts section; bread basket

PROCEDURE

Sit in a circle on the floor with the bread in front of the teacher.

Teacher: Today you all shared the work of making this beautiful loaf of bread. What shape is the bread? (heart) What does a heart remind us of? (love) Who will eat this bread? (all) The heart shape reminds us that God loves us. We break this bread apart so everyone can have a piece. *(Break bread and place in basket.)* This reminds us that God wants us to share his love with each other, just as we share this bread with each other.

Listen now to this prayer: Thank you, God, for your love and for the food we eat. Help us to share your love and your gifts with everyone. Amen. Please take some bread and pass the basket to your neighbor. *(Share bread and conversation.)*

RESPONSE PRAYER

Teacher: Loving God, you share your love with all of us. Help us to share with others. When we are on the playground,
Children: help us to share.
Teacher: When we play with friends,
Children: help us to share.
Teacher: When we are at home,
Children: help us to share.
Teacher: When our friends are sad,
Children: help us to share.

REPEAT PRAYER

PROCEDURE

Children repeat after teacher:
God of love,/ thank you for people/ who share with us./ Help us/ to share with others./ Amen.

Music

Bob's Favorite Street Songs. 7502104144.
> (A & M Records Inc., P.O. Box 118, Hollywood, CA 90078).
> "Somebody Come and Play"

Hi, God! 27260.
> (North American Liturgy Resources, 2110 W. Peoria Ave., Phoenix, AZ 85029).
> "What Makes Love Grow?"

In Harmony. BSK 3481.
> (Sesame Street Records, 1 Lincoln Plaza, New York, NY 10023).
> "A Friend for All Seasons"
> "Share"

The Music Machine. BWR 2004.
> (Sparrow Records, 8587 Canoga Ave., Canoga Park, CA 91304).
> "Joy"

Numbers! C - 5079.
> (Children's Television Workshop, 1 Lincoln Plaza, New York, NY 10023).
> "One and One Make Two"

Books

Cohen, Miriam. *Don't Eat Too Much Turkey*. New York: Greenwillow Books, 1987.

Cotton, Debie. *Messy Marcy MacIntyre*. Milwaukee: Gareth Stevens Children's Books, 1991.

Conford, Ellen. *Just the Thing for Geraldine*. Boston: Little, Brown & Co., 1974.

Delton, Judy. *Two Good Friends*. New York: Crown Publishers, 1974.

deLynan, Alicia. *It's Mine!* New York: Dial Books for Young Readers, 1988.

dePaola, Tomie. *Watch Out for the Chicken Feet in Your Soup*. Englewood Cliffs, N.J.: Prentice Hall, 1974.

Dragonwood, Crescent. *This Is the Bread I Baked for Ned*. New York: Macmillan Publishing Co., 1989.

Goldin, Barbara. *Just Enough Is Plenty*. New York: Viking Kestrel, 1988.

Gould, Deborah. *Brendan's Best-Timed Birthday*. New York: Bradbury, 1988.

Harper, Anita, and Susan Hellard. *What Feels Best?* New York: G.P. Putnam's Sons, 1988.

Hayward, Linda. *Mine!* New York: Random House, 1988.

Hutchins, Pat. *The Door Bell Rang*. New York: Greenwillow Books, 1986.

Keats, Ezra Jack. *Peter's Chair*. New York: Harper & Row, 1967.

Lionni, Leo. *It's Mine!* New York: Alfred A. Knopf, 1986.

Polacco, Pat. *The Keeping Quilt*. New York: Simon & Schuster, 1988.

Purdy, Carol. *Least of All*. New York: M.K. McElderry Books, 1987.

Riddell, Chris. *Ben and the Bear*. New York: J.B. Lippincott, 1986.

Vincent, Gabrielle. *Ernest and Celestine*. New York: Greenwillow Books, 1981.

Williams, Vera B. *Cherries and Cherry Pits*. New York: Greenwillow Books, 1986.

Ziefert, Harriet. *Me, Too! Me, Too!* New York: Harper & Row, 1988.

Parent Page

Ideas for things to do with your child and family to promote sharing:

Share looking out a window on a rainy or snowy day.

Go on a treasure hunt in your yard or in a park. Share your "treasures."

Make a Sharing Salad. Let each family member choose a fruit or vegetable and chop it up. Put all the pieces in one bowl, mix, and share.

Choose a favorite book. Read it together.

Share a joke.

Ask your child to teach you a song. Sing it together.

Share your time with someone who's sick.

Take care of a garden or house plants together.

Use a blanket and some chairs to build a tent. Sit in it together. Share feelings.

Share stories about when you were a child.

Share prayer before meals, in the morning, and at night.

Make treats together to share at school.

Share picking up toys.

Go on an autumn walk. Crunch the leaves. Rake the leaves into piles and jump in them.

Share blessings. Make the sign of the cross on each other's forehead at bedtime.

Share with those who need help. Donate toys, clothes, or food to a homeless shelter.

Share cleaning up the kitchen after a meal.

Have a Christmas ornament-making day. Make a few extra ornaments for shut-in members of your church.

Share your faith. Use God-talk with your child.

Give a hug and a smile to every family member every day.

"A child is a guest in the house, to be loved and respected,
never possessed, since he (she) belongs to God." — J.D. Salinger

CHAPTER 6

HELPING

Discussion

BACKGROUND

Hebrew Scripture records accounts of God helping the people over and over again. In Christian Scripture, we see Jesus continually helping others. To help is to model the behavior of God.

Through the parable of the Good Samaritan, Jesus teaches us that help and love are closely related. A Mr. Rogers song uses examples of people helping others to show that "there are many ways to say, 'I love you.'" When we give help, we enable people to meet basic needs, but we also give them, and ourselves, a sense of worth. By helping, we put love into action.

Because children are quick to model what they see and experience, adults can encourage children to become good helpers by making them aware and appreciative of the many people who help them in different ways. Give children opportunities to be helpful in class and teach them skills that will enable them to be helpful. Suggest ways they can be helpful at home and in their community. Commend their helpful actions. Being successful at helping will give them a sense of being needed and of having value and will nurture their desire to become the helpful people God calls them to be.

QUESTIONS

Who in your family helps you? How do they help? How does that make you feel?

Who in your neighborhood helps you? How? What do you say to someone who helps?

Why do you think God gives you so many people to help you? (Lead the children to understand that helping is a way to show love.)

What do you do to help your family?

How do you help your friends?

What are some things you can do to help at school?

How do you help to take care of God's world?

How do you feel when you help?

Discovery Centers

Sorting Center

CHILDREN WILL
> touch items
> sort items
> co-operate on a job
> accomplish a task
> be helpful

MATERIALS
> 1 tray with a pile of screws, nails, and washers and 3 containers; 1 tray with a pile of paper clips, rubber bands, and brads and 3 containers

PROCEDURE
> Work in teams of 3 or 4. Sort and place like objects in the same container.

I Can Help

CHILDREN WILL
> button, zip, and snap
> practice a skill
> help a friend get dressed
> accomplish a task
> receive affirmation

MATERIALS
> Child-sized shirt with buttons, jacket with zipper, cap with snap

PROCEDURE
> Work in pairs. One person pretends to be the "child" and the other is the "helper." The "helper" assists the "child" in putting on and fastening an article of clothing. The "child" thanks the "helper." Reverse roles.

Helper Matching

CHILDREN WILL
> look at pictures of many neighborhood helpers
> identify helpers
> match tools to helpers

MATERIALS
> Pictures of neighborhood helpers (police, doctors, grocers, teachers, firefighters, carpenters, etc.) Cards illustrating tools used by helpers (police badge, cash register, books, hose, hammer, etc.)

PROCEDURE

Match tools to the helpers who use them. Mix them up when you are finished so another person can work with them.

Snack Center

CHILDREN WILL

prepare a snack
practice a skill
do something for the class
accomplish a task
be helpful

MATERIALS

Soda crackers; peanut butter; plastic knives; large tray; napkins

PROCEDURE

Spread peanut butter on 4 crackers. Arrange the crackers on the tray. At snack time, all will share the crackers.

What Can I Use?

CHILDREN WILL

look at object cards
decide what tools would help them do a job
name the tools
match the tool pictures to the object the tools could make

MATERIALS

Object cards, i.e., pictures of a greeting card, a birdhouse, cookies, etc.; tool cards, i.e., pictures of markers, crayons, scissors, hammer, nails, saw, spoon, bowl, cookie sheet, oven, etc.

PROCEDURE

Look at the object card. Choose and name the tools you would use to make the object. Place the appropriate tool pictures below each object card.

Crafts
Helping Hand Centerpiece

CHILDREN WILL
> cut and glue
> make something for their family
> choose jobs they will do at home

MATERIALS
> Markers; glue; for each child: toilet paper roll covered with white paper; paper hand, 4 1/2" long with a 2 1/2" long arm attatched; paper heart; six 1 1/2 x 11" paper job strips.

PROCEDURE
> (Teacher preparation: Print sample jobs, i.e., I WILL FEED OUR PET, I WILL SET THE TABLE, I WILL PICK UP MY TOYS, etc. Make copies and cut apart. On each heart, print: PLEASE PICK A JOB/FOR ME TO DO./ I'LL BE A GOOD/HELPER FOR YOU. Trace hands.) Cut out hands. Glue heart on hand. Fold arm back at wrist. Glue hand to upright toilet paper roll. Tuck arm up into bottom of roll, making a floor for the cylinder. Choose 6 job strips. Fold and place inside the roll. Give to your family. Let them choose a job for you to do every day.

Dust Mitt

CHILDREN WILL
> lace
> make a useful tool

MATERIALS
> Hole punch; for each child: 2 felt mitten-shaped hands and 2 pieces of yarn

PROCEDURE
> (Teacher preparation: Cut out 2 hands for each child. Punch holes around the edge of the hands, except at the wrist, making sure the holes on the 2 hands line up. Make knots at 1 end of each piece of yarn.) Lace up 1 side of the hands, stopping at the top center. Lace up the other side. Tie the yarn together at the top. Take home. Dust something.

Star Helper Award

CHILDREN WILL
> identify a helper
> affirm a helper
> make an award
> present an award

Patterns for Helping Hand Centerpiece

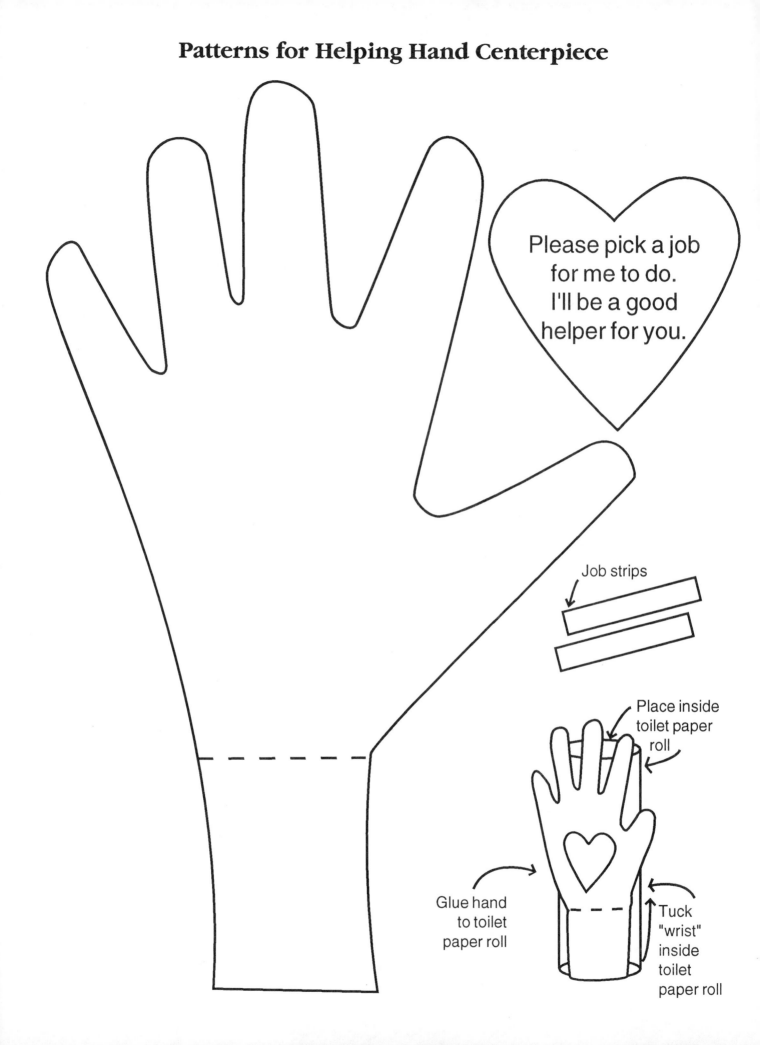

Please pick a job for me to do. I'll be a good helper for you.

Job strips

Place inside toilet paper roll

Glue hand to toilet paper roll

Tuck "wrist" inside toilet paper roll

MATERIALS

Markers; glitter; glue; for each child: large poster board star with (*blank*) IS A STAR HELPER printed on it.

PROCEDURE

Think of someone in your church, school, or family who is a very good helper. Print that person's name on the star. Decorate the star. Give the star award to your special helper.

Helper Code Card

CHILDREN WILL

identify someone they can help
glue (or draw) and make a handprint
write a sentence in code
give the message to someone

MATERIALS

Markers; poster paint; brush; for each child: 1 piece of light colored construction paper; picture of eye; picture of tin can

PROCEDURE

(Teacher preparation: With the 11 1/2" side of the paper as the base, print DEAR *[blank]* In the upper left and LOVE, *[blank]* in the lower right.) Print the name of a person you can help. Print your name after the word "Love." Arrange the following symbols from left to right as in a sentence: eye (glue on the picture or draw one), tin can, hand print (Paint your palm and press on the paper), a "U." (The code is translated: "I can help you.") Give the card to a person you can help. See if they can break the code and read the message. Help them do something.

Helper Code Card

Dear _____

Love, _____

Movement

Helper Chant

PROCEDURE

Put hands on hips and march in a row as you chant:

Bus drivers, store keepers, police people, too!
Working hard for me and you!

(change direction)

Firefighters, doctors, teachers and more —
They work in an office, factory or store!

(stand still; clap on each letter)

H - E - L ——— P - E - R !

(reach to the ceiling on each word)

Helpers! Helpers!

(applaud as you yell)

That's what they are! Hooray for helpers!

Helpers Do

MATERIALS

Box containing names of helpers, i.e., doctor, bus driver, baker, mom, big brother, etc.

PROCEDURE

Sit in a circle. Pass cigar box around as you sing the following song (tune: "Here We Go 'Round the Mulberry Bush"):

Helpers, they help me every day, every day, every day;
Helpers, they help me every day;
And here is how a *(name a helper)* helps.

The child who has the box on the last line opens it and removes a name. Read the name and ask, "Who knows how a *(blank)* helps?" The child who opened the box chooses someone to tell or pantomime the answer. Begin the song again. If the box stops at someone who has already had a turn, pass it to the left until it reaches someone who has not.

Missing Persons Department

MATERIALS

Flannel board; felt-backed pictures of community helpers

PROCEDURE

Each child chooses a picture of a community helper. As the teacher reads a description of the "missing person," the children act like detectives and listen for clues that will describe the person in the picture they're holding. When they hear the correct description, they run and place their picture on the flannel board. (Sample description: I'm thinking of someone who wears a shiny badge. This person might have a whistle. You might see this person helping children cross the street.) After everyone has posted a picture, mix up the pictures and play again.

Help! Help! Helper!

MATERIALS

"I Need Help" situation cards, i.e., "I lost my lunch money," "My grocery bag ripped," "I spilled my milk," "My books fell in the mud" etc.; cassette recording of "I'm a Very Good Helper" (see Procedure); tape recorder

PROCEDURE

(Teacher preparation: Tape record the children singing this song: [tune: "This Little Light of Mine"] "I'm a very good helper/I help whenever I can./ I'm a very good helper/ I help whenever I can./ I'm a very good helper/ I help whenever I can./ I can help/ I can help/ I can help.")

Stand and form a large circle. 1 child is "it." "It" walks around the outside of the circle, tapping each person on the shoulder while the music plays. When the music stops, "it" takes the last person he (she) touched into the center of the circle to be the "Helper." Everyone else sits down. "It" draws a situation card. The "Helper" must tell or pantomime how to help. After the "Helper" has offered a suggestion, everyone stands up. "It" joins the circle, and the "Helper" becomes "it." Continue the game until all have had a turn.

Prayer

Prayer Activity

Teacher: God of goodness and love, you give us many helpers. Here are some that we are especially thankful for:

Child: I'm thankful for *(name)* because he (she) helps me *(blank)*.

(As each child names someone, the teacher prints the name on a large piece of posterboard or fabric. After all the children have had a turn to name someone, the names are displayed and the teacher continues.)

Teacher: How happy we are, God, to have so many people to help us. We thank you for them all.

Children repeat after teacher: Please bless/all the people/who help me./ Amen.

RESPONSE PRAYER

Teacher: Dear loving God, when someone says, "Please pick up your toys,"
Children: help me to be a good helper.
Teacher: When someone says, "Please hang up your clothes,"
Children: help me to be a good helper.
Teacher: When someone says, "Please feed our pet,"
Children: help me to be a good helper.
Teacher: When someone says, "Please take out the trash,"
Children: help me to be a good helper.
All: We want to be good helpers, God. Please show us the way. Amen.

REPEAT PRAYER

PROCEDURE

Children repeat after teacher:
Loving God,/ thank you for all the people/who help me./ Help me to be/a good helper, too./ Amen.

Music

Free to Be a Family: Marlo Thomas and Friends. CS5196.
    (A & M Records, Inc., P.O. Box 118, Hollywood, CA 90078).
    "Thank Someone"

People in Your Neighborhood. CTW 22092.
    (Children's Television Network, 1 Lincoln Plaza, New York, NY 10023).
    "The People in Your Neighborhood"

A Place of Our Own. MRN 8104.
    (Family Communications, Inc., 4802 Fifth Ave., Pittsburgh, PA 15213).
    "I Need You"
    "Many Ways to Say I Love You"

Songs for the Wonder of God Series: Celebrate! 2322-8.
    (Raven Music (BMI), 4107 Woodland Park Ave. N., Seattle, WA 98103.
    "You Are My Helpers"

You Are Special. MRN 8103.
    (Family Communications, Inc., 4802 Fifth Ave., Pittsburgh, PA 15213).
    "You've Got to Do It"
    "You Have to Learn Your Trade"

Books

Ancona, George. *Helping Out*. New York: Ticknor & Fields, 1985.

Arnold, Caroline. *Who Is Keeping Us Healthy?* New York: Franklin Watts, 1982.

Arnold, Caroline. *Who Works Here?* New York: Franklin Watts, 1982.

Buerger, Jane, and Jennie Davis. *Helping: What Is It?* Elgin, Ill.: Child's World, 1984, rev.

Clifton, Lucille. *My Friend Jacob*. New York: E.P. Dutton, 1980.

Delton, Judy. *Two Good Friends*. New York: Crown Publishers, 1974.

Florian, Douglas. *People Working*. New York: Thomas Y. Crowell, 1983.

Galdone, Paul. *The Elves and the Shoemaker*. New York: Clarion Books, 1984.

Green, Norma. *Hole in the Dike*. New York: Thomas Y. Crowell, 1974.

Greene, Laura. *Help: Getting to Know About Needing and Giving*. New York: Human Sciences Press, 1987.

Mahy, Margaret. *Keeping House*. New York: Margaret McElderry Books, 1991.

Merriam, Eve. *Mommies at Work*. New York: Simon & Schuster, 1989.

Rockwell, Anne. *Handy Hank Will Fix It*. New York: Henry Holt & Co., 1988.

Rockwell, Anne. *Nice and Clean*. New York: Macmillan, 1984.

Rylant, Cynthia. *Mr. Grigg's Work*. New York: Orchard Books, 1989.

Simon, Norma. *I'm Busy, Too*. Chicago: Albert Whitman & Co., 1980.

Stevens, Janet. *Androcles and the Lion*. New York: Holiday House, 1989.

Williams, Barbara. *Someday, Said Mitchell*. New York: E.P. Dutton, 1976.

Williams, Vera B. *Music, Music for Everyone*. New York: Greenwillow Books, 1984.

Zemach, Margot. *The Little Red Hen*. New York: Farrar, Straus, & Giroux, 1983.

Parent Page

Ideas for things to do for and with your child and family to foster a helping attitude:

Begin your day by asking God to help you be a cheerful helper.

Make your child responsible for a specific job to help the family.

Post a family job chart. Rotate jobs.

Play restaurant. Let your child serve food or wash dishes.

Make a job jar. Let everyone put in job suggestions and draw one out and do it each week.

Clean a closet together. Celebrate a completed job with a favorite snack.

Honor family helpers at meal time. Tell what they did to help the family.

Teach your child a new skill that will enable him (her) to be more helpful.

Hold a Super Saturday Clean-Up Day. Have the whole family help. Vote on an enjoyable activity to do together afterward.

Award a "Helper's Day Off" to one family member each month. Help that person relax by doing his (her) chores.

Mail a thank you letter to a community helper for a job well done.

Divide the work for an entire meal—planning, shopping, preparing, serving, and clean-up—among family members.

Thank a teacher for helping you to learn something.

Help a neighbor with a chore.

Take care of a pet or a plant.

Help someone without being asked.

Pick up litter around your school.

Help to spring clean your church for Easter.

Read a book about someone who is a good helper.

In your evening prayers, thank God for all the people who help you.

"I will help you, says the Lord." — Isaiah 41:14

CHAPTER 7

Thanking

Discussion

BACKGROUND

"It is right and just to give God thanks," prays the entire church through the eucharistic prayer. Holy Scripture teaches us to thank God "for God is good." It is never too early to teach children to say "thank you" or to make them aware that it is God whom we thank for all our gifts.

Developing a thankful attitude helps children to grow both spiritually and socially. Thankful people are able to look beyond themselves to see the worth of others and the connectiveness of all things. Thankful hearts open out, welcoming and affirming others, appreciating gifts received, reciprocating generosity.

Teach children to be thankful by your own example. Verbalize your thanks to God, to others, and to the children for their kind and helpful deeds. Help them to be aware of the many things people do for them and encourage them to say "thank you." Acknowledge their thankful behavior. Tell them that showing their appreciation can make others feel happy.

Give them opportunities to thank God through prayer, songs, and crafts. Remind the children that we also thank God by doing what God asks us to do.

QUESTIONS

What are some things God made?

Who did God give those things to?

What do you say to God for giving you these gifts?

How could you show you are thankful for God's gifts?

What do you think God wants you to do with these gifts?

What are some things your family gives you?

How do you show you are thankful? How do they feel when you say "thank you"?

What are some things you give to others?

How do you feel when someone thanks you for sharing, helping, or being kind?

Discovery Centers

Thank You Post Office

CHILDREN WILL

> print the name of a person they want to thank
> draw a picture of what they are thanking someone for
> print their own name
> put their "letter" in an envelope, address and stamp it
> "mail" their letter
> deliver their letter

MATERIALS

> Letter forms, envelopes, decorative stamps, pencils, markers, mail box

PROCEDURE

> (Teacher preparation: Make letter forms by printing DEAR *(blank)*, THANK YOU FOR *(leave a large space for drawing)*. LOVE, *(blank)*." Decorate a box to use as the mail box.) Print the name of someone you want to thank. Draw a picture of what you want to thank them for. Print your own name. Fold your letter, put it in an envelope, stick on a stamp, and print the name of the person it is for. (Be sure to include a last name). Print your name on the other side of the envelope. Put it in the mail box. The teacher will deliver the letters to the children before they go home, so they can deliver them to the addressees.

Message Mountain

CHILDREN WILL

> arrange boxes according to size
> co-operate in stacking boxes
> say "thank you" to co-workers
> read a thank you prayer
> accomplish a task

MATERIALS

> 13 different sized flat boxes; wrapping paper; markers

PROCEDURE

> (Teacher preparation: Wrap boxes. Beginning with the smallest and going to the largest, print one capital letter on the side of each to spell out THANK YOU, GOD! Be sure to include the two blank boxes needed for spaces between words. Mix up the boxes.) Form a team of 3 or 4 children. Co-operate in building a mountain by placing the largest box on the bottom, then the next largest, and so on until the smallest is on top. Say "thank you" to each other as you position the boxes. Read the message on the mountain.

Wreath of Thanks
(A version of "Husker Du?" for 2 - 6 children)

CHILDREN WILL

play a game
take turns
name things we thank God for
practice memory skills

MATERIALS

20 paper circles, 2" diameter, all the same color; 10 pairs of small pictures of God's gifts (Note: card and gift catalogues are a good source); posterboard, marker

PROCEDURE

(Teacher preparation: Glue 1 picture on each circle, or draw pictures if you prefer, so that you have 10 sets of matching pictures. Make the game board by drawing 20 circles on the posterboard to form a large wreath. Inside the wreath, print, "Thank you, God, for all your gifts.") Spread out all the circles, picture side down. The first child picks up a circle and says, "Thank you, God, for *(name what is pictured)*." The same child picks up another circle, hoping to get a match. If there is a match, the pair of circles are placed in the wreath on the game board. If there is no match, the circles are re-entered into the playing field. Either way, the turn passes to the next person. Set a time limit for the game. See how many circles the group as a whole can get onto the wreath.

Crafts

"Bee" Thankful Magnet

CHILDREN WILL

glue and tape to make a magnet

take the magnet home as a reminder to be thankful

MATERIALS

Glue; tape; markers; for each child: 1 yellow paper circle (2 $\frac{1}{2}$" diam.) for head; 1 yellow paper oval (2 $\frac{3}{4}$" x 3 $\frac{1}{2}$") for body; black paper oval (1" x 2 $\frac{1}{2}$") for neck; two 3" and four 6" pieces of black pipe cleaner; 2 white notebook reinforcers; two 5" long white paper wings; two 1" strips of self-sticking magnet tape

PROCEDURE

(Teacher preparation: Print BEE THANKFUL on each body.) Glue neck (placed horizontally) to bottom of head and top of body. Stick 2 reinforcers on head to make eyes. Draw mouth. Shape antennae out of 2 short pipe cleaners and tape to back of head. Shape arms and legs out of 4 long pipe cleaners. Tape arms to back of neck. Tape legs to back of body. Tape wings behind arms. Stick magnet tape to back of head and body.

Thanking Cross

CHILDREN WILL

decorate and cut letters

glue letters to make a cross

make a symbol that reminds them to thank God

MATERIALS

Markers; glue; scissors; for each child: one 2" wide, 8 $\frac{1}{2}$" x 11" cross, cut from poster board; 1 sheet of ten 1 $\frac{1}{2}$" squares with an open block letter in each, to include 2 T's, 2 H's, 2 N's, 2 K's, 1 A, 1 heart

PROCEDURE

(Tell the children the cross reminds us of Jesus, the heart reminds us that Jesus loves us, and the words they will glue on remind us to thank God for his gifts.) Color and decorate block letters. Cut out squares. Glue "A" at the center of cross. Glue the other letters to spell "thank" horizontally and vertically. Glue heart to the bottom of cross. Take home and display.

Thank You Gift—Notes 'n' Things

CHILDREN WILL

identify someone to thank

sew and glue

make and give a useful thank you gift

Patterns for "Bee" Thankful Magnet

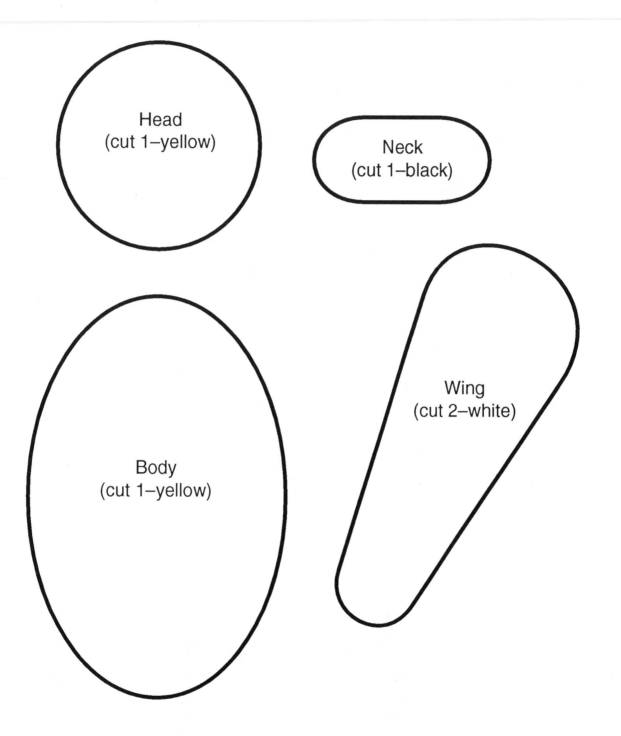

Head
(cut 1–yellow)

Neck
(cut 1–black)

Wing
(cut 2–white)

Body
(cut 1–yellow)

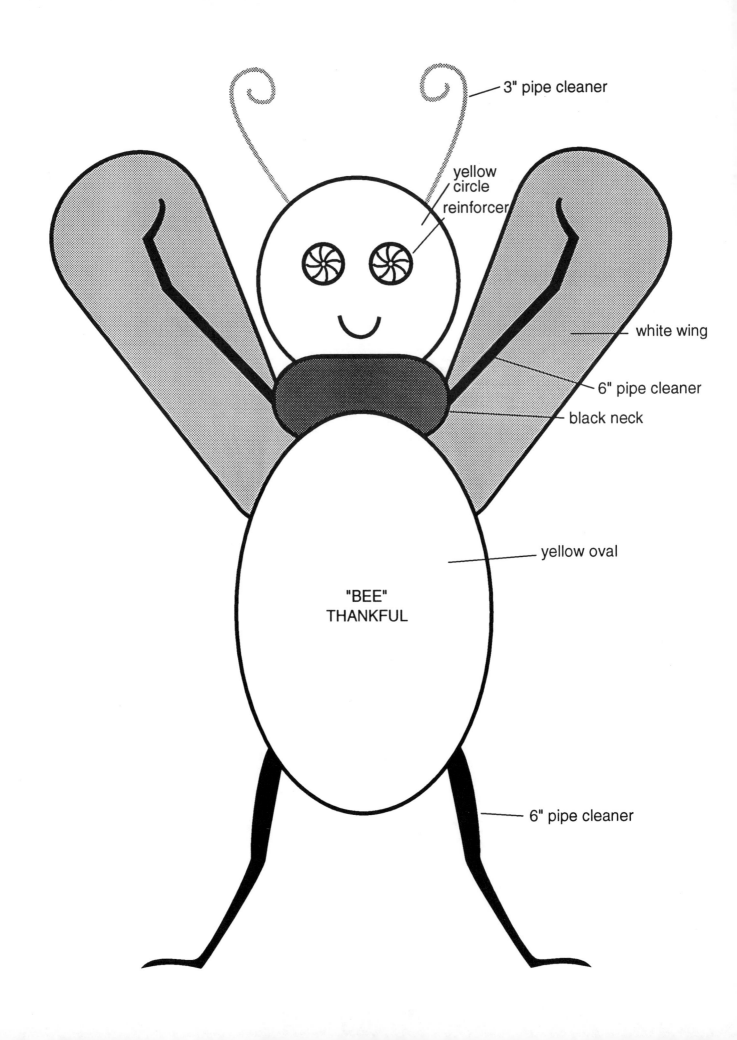

MATERIALS

Paper punch; glue; pictures of flowers, animals, etc.; for each child: 1 whole and one half 9" styrofoam plate; 28" yarn; 12" yarn; paper heart

PROCEDURE

(Teacher preparation: Print on hearts: "I made this little gift for you/ To thank you for the things you do./ Each time you use it, think of me/ Saying, 'Thank you, thank you,' sincerely." Line up the half plate and the lower half of the whole plate, forming a pocket. Punch holes $1/2$" apart around their perimeter. Punch 1 hole at the top.) Use the long yarn to lash the 2 plates together. Use the short yarn to make a loop at the top. Glue the heart on the pocket. Glue on pictures. Take home. Give to someone you want to thank.

Thank-u-Gram

CHILDREN WILL

identify someone to thank
identify a reason to thank someone
make and deliver a written statement of thanks

MATERIALS

For each child: glue; sheet of rectangles with word choices: "Thank," "you," "for," "helping," "loving," "reading," "cooking," "hugging," "to," "with," "me," etc.; 1 piece of 8 $1/2$" x 11" onion skin paper; scissors

PROCEDURE

Decide who you want to thank and why. Cut out words that explain your reasons. Glue the words on onion skin to make a sentence. Let dry. Fold. Deliver your thank-u-gram.

Movement

Thank You, God
(An action verse)

PROCEDURE

Do movements as you say this verse:

For hoppity rabbits with wiggly noses *(hop, wiggle nose)*;
For sunshine *(make a circle with hands)*, and rainbows *("draw" a rainbow in the air)*, and pretty roses *(smell roses)*;
For friends who play and make me glad *(shake hands, smile)*;
For people to hug when I am sad *(hug self, frown)*;
For me, myself *(point to self)* and all I'll be *(extend arms outward)*;
I thank you, God *(hands folded in prayer)*, most lovingly *(hand on heart, offer upwards)*.

Thank-You-Kindly Circle Dance

PROCEDURE

Choose partners. Form a large circle with everyone facing the same direction so the circle will move counter-clockwise. The teacher gives an example of someone helping, i.e., "Dad packed my lunch today," and asks, "What do we say to Dad?" The partners hold hands and skip around the circle as they sing (tune: "She'll Be Coming 'Round the Mountain"):

Oh, we all say, "Thank you, kindly, for your gift!"
Oh, we all say, "Thank you, kindly, for your gift!"
Oh, we all say, "Thank you, kindly; Oh, we all say, "Thank you, kindly";
Oh, we all say, "Thank you, kindly for your gift!"

Teacher asks, "What was Dad's gift?" After someone answers, change partners and face the opposite direction. The teacher gives another example and the dance begins again.

Thanking Chant/Clap

PROCEDURE

Clap on something different (thighs, arms, desk, floor, etc.) after the first 2 lines of each verse. Clap 3 times on the last line of each verse:

We thank you in the morning! *(clap)* We thank you in the night! *(clap)*
We thank you in the darkness and the broad day light! *(3 claps)*

We thank you in the sunshine! *(clap)* We thank you in the rain! *(clap)*
We thank you and we want to say it over again! *(3 claps)*

Thank-ful Race

MATERIALS

3 oz. paper cup with 1 oz. of water; pitcher of water; stopwatch or timer

PROCEDURE

Divide children into 2 groups. Form 2 lines, facing each other, at opposite ends of the room. The object of the game is to pass the cup of water, relay style, to all the children in a given amount of time. The first person in line "A" carries it to the first person in line "B" who carries it to the second person in line "A" and so on. If the water is spilled, the cup is taken to the teacher who refills it. (The clock does not stop.) Before the cup can be passed, the receiver *must* say, "Thank you." If the "thank you" is omitted, everyone in both lines must sit down and say, "Thank you" 10 times. (The clock does not stop.) The whole class wins when it beats the clock.

Prayer

Prayer Activity

MATERIALS

   26 index cards, with a letter of the alphabet printed on each; 26 small objects or pictures, each representing an initial letter; large blue paper circle with continent shapes drawn on to represent the world

PROCEDURE

   (Teacher preparation: Hide all the objects.) Take a letter. Search for something that starts with that letter. After finding it, take it and your card and sit in a circle around the world. When everyone is ready, go through the alphabet, taking a turn to say, "We are thankful for (*name object found*)." Place your object on the blue circle; give your card to the teacher. After everything is on the world, the teacher says, "Look how full the world is of God's gifts!" Everyone cheers: "Thank you, God!"

RESPONSE PRAYER

Teacher: God gives us a beautiful world and many people who love and care for us. Sometimes we get busy or tired and forget to say thank you. Let's ask God to help us remember:

When our friends share,
Children: help us remember to say "thank you."
Teacher: When our parents feed us,
Children: help us remember to say "thank you."
Teacher: When we see a butterfly or a beautiful sunset,
Children: help us remember to say "thank you."

REPEAT PRAYER

PROCEDURE

   Children repeat after teacher:
   Loving God,/ you are so good to us./ You give us all your love./ We thank you./ Amen.

Music

Close Your Eyes. . .I Got a Surprise. FH09.
        (Fontaine House, 7404 Mason Ave., Chicago, IL 60638).
        "Thanks For the Chance"

Free to Be a Family: Marlo Thomas and Friends. CS5196.
        (A & M Records, Inc., P.O. Box 118, Hollywood, CA 90078).
        "Thank Someone"

Hi, God! 27260.
        (North American Liturgy Resources, 2110 W. Peoria Ave., Phoenix, AZ 85029).
        "Hi, God!"
        "Thank You, Lord"

Hi, God 2. 27262.
        (North American Liturgy Resources, 2110 W. Peoria Ave., Phoenix, AZ 85029).
        "All Your Gifts of Life"

Travellin' with Ella Jenkins. FC 7640.
        (Folkways Records & Service Corp., 43 W. 61st St., New York, NY 10023).
        "Thank You" (in several different languages)

Books

Baynes, Pauline. *Thanks Be to God*. New York: Macmillan, 1990.

Behrens, June. *The Manners Book*. Chicago: Children's Press, 1980.

Berenstain, Stan and Jan. *The Berenstain Bears Forget Their Manners*. New York: Random House, 1985.

Bunting, Eve. *How Many Days to America?* New York: Clarion Books, 1988.

Dellinger, Annetta. *Hugging*. Elgin, Ill.: Child's World, 1985.

Goldin, Barbara. *Just Enough Is Plenty*. New York: Viking Kestrel, 1988.

Hallinan, P.K. *I'm Thankful Each Day*. Chicago: Children's Press, 1981.

McDonnell, Janet. *Thankfulness*. Elgin, Ill.: Child's World, 1988.

Moncure, Jane. *I Never Say I'm Thankful, But I Am*. Elgin, Ill.: Child's World, 1979.

Moncure, Jane. *Please. . . Thanks. . . I'm Sorry*. Elgin, Ill.: Child's World, 1985.

Moncure, Jane. *Thank You, God, for Fall*. Elgin, Ill.: Child's World, 1979.

Moncure, Jane. *Thank You, God, for Spring*. Elgin, Ill.: Child's World, 1979.

Moncure, Jane. *Thank You, God, for Summer*. Elgin, Ill.: Child's World, 1979.

Moncure, Jane. *Thank You, God, for Winter*. Elgin, Ill.: Child's World, 1979.

Munro, Leaf. *Manners Can Be Fun*. New York: J.B. Lippincott, 1985.

Parrish, Peggy. *Mind Your Manners*. New York: Greenwillow Books, 1978.

Parrish, Peggy. *Thank You, Amelia Bedelia*. New York: HarperCollins Publishers, 1992.

Reece, Colleen. *Saying Thank You*. Elgin, Ill.: Child's World, 1982.

Riehecky, Janet. *"Thank You."* Chicago: Children's Press, 1989.

Scarry, Richard. *Richard Scarry's Please and Thank You Book*. New York: Random House, 1978.

Parent Page

Ideas for things to do for and with your child and family to foster a thankful attitude:

Smile in the morning to show your thanks for a new day.

Thank God for your talents by sharing them with others.

Stay after Mass to thank the priest for his service.

Have all family members write a letter to an out of town relative or friend thanking them for their love.

Find a psalm of thanks in the Bible and share it with your family.

Take a treat to a neighbor to say, "Thanks for being a good neighbor."

Go fruit picking. Sit outside and eat what you picked. Thank God for this delicious gift.

Thank someone for helping you by offering to help him (her).

Go to church with your family and give thanks together with other parish families.

Tell each family member why you are thankful for him (her).

Give thanks for all you have by sharing with the poor.

Hug your child and express your thanks for his (her) birth.

Try to find something to be thankful for during a sad time.

Fly a kite. Thank God for the wind.

Sit outdoors. Look in the four directions and up and down. Thank God for something you see each time.

Take time after Mass to thank the choir members and musicians.

Talk about someone who's dead. Tell what you thank them for.

Thank a friend for sharing a toy or coming to play.

Make saying "thank you" a habit for everyone in the family.

Thank your teacher for teaching you something.

"Give thanks to the Lord, for he is good." — Psalm 106:1

CHAPTER 8

FORGIVING

Discussion

BACKGROUND

How unbearable life would be without forgiveness. Our human failures can make us feel worthless and unloved, but we are freed from this condition because we are forgiven. When we turn to God in repentance, Jesus tells us, we are *always* forgiven. What is more, as we learn through the parables of the Good Shepherd and the Prodigal Son, and especially through Jesus' own death on the cross, we are forgiven because God loves us so much!

Use role-playing, stories, puppets, and drawing to help children understand that when they do something unkind, they have sad feelings and when they are forgiven, they are happy again. Teach them that saying "I'm sorry" helps them and the other person to feel happy again.

Children learn about God's loving forgiveness by experiencing it. Forgiveness can't be offered, then, in a triumphal "I-told-you-so" manner. It must be given as God gives it: joyfully because "one who was lost is now found." Your tone of voice, facial expressions, body language, and attitude while forgiving someone will teach a child more about forgiveness than countless religion lessons will. Experiencing the joy of forgiveness will move children to want to offer it to others.

QUESTIONS

What are some things that brothers and sisters and friends argue about?

How does arguing make people feel?

What have you done to make someone feel sad?

How did that make you feel?

What did you do to make that person feel better?

How did you feel then?

If you make someone feel sad, what should you say to them?

What else could you do?

If someone makes you sad and then tells you, "I'm sorry," what could you say to them?

Discovery Centers

Forgive Solitaire

CHILDREN WILL

    sort pictures and letters

    match letters

    spell out "I can forgive"

MATERIALS

    24 "playing cards" made from heavy paper or wrapping paper; clear contact paper; large heart-shaped board with I CAN FORGIVE in the center

PROCEDURE

    (Teacher preparation: Print 1 letter of I CAN FORGIVE on 11 cards. Draw a heart on the remaining 13 cards. Cover with clear contact. Mix up cards.) Place all cards in a stack, face down. Count 1, 2, 3 cards. Turn the 3rd card face up. If it is a letter, place it on the matching letter on the board. The player wins when all the letters on the board are covered. (Note: For 2 children to play, divide the deck and take turns.)

I "Can" Forgive

CHILDREN WILL

    toss bean bags into can

    see I CAN FORGIVE message printed on can

    reinforce positive message by getting bags in can

MATERIALS

    Large can with I CAN FORGIVE printed on it; 3 bean bags or nerf balls

PROCEDURE

    Take turns trying to get bean bags into can. Everyone gets 3 tries.

Forgiveness Maze

CHILDREN WILL

    walk through a maze

    say "I'm sorry" and "I forgive"

    give and receive a hug

MATERIALS

    String or yarn; tape

PROCEDURE

    (Teacher preparation: Make a maze with string. Form 4 squares of different sizes, 1 within the other, each with several openings. Secure with tape.) 1 child stands in the center and is the "Forgiver." Another child walks through the maze, searching for forgiveness. No lines may be crossed. When the searcher reaches the center, he (she) says "I'm sorry," and the person in the center says "I forgive." Both hug.

Sorry/Forgive Keys

CHILDREN WILL
> match keys
> read "I'm sorry" and "I forgive"

MATERIALS
> 6 pairs of paper keys, each pair slightly different than the others; clear contact paper; markers; scissors

PROCEDURE
> (Teacher preparation: Print I'M SORRY on 1 key and I FORGIVE on the other key in each set. Cover with clear contact paper. Mix up all the keys.) Find matching keys to form 6 pairs. Read what is on each key as you match them.

Forgiving Hearts

CHILDREN WILL
> hold and drop straws
> pick up forgiving heart straws
> count forgiving hearts to measure success

MATERIALS
> 24 drinking straws; 10 tiny paper hearts; tape

PROCEDURE
> (Teacher preparation: Tape hearts on 10 straws. Tell the children that the heart stands for love and forgiveness.) Play as you play pick up sticks. The object is to see how many forgiving heart straws you can get without moving the others. Count your forgiving hearts. Try to do better the next time you play.

Crafts

Good Shepherd

CHILDREN WILL

glue pieces and assemble "Good Shepherd" figure
make a reminder of a forgiving person

MATERIALS

Markers; glue; for each child: toilet paper roll; 4 1/2" x 7" fabric; construction paper arms and hands; 7" twig; 2" styrofoam ball; rubber band; 8" square of fabric

PROCEDURE

(Teacher preparation: Glue 1 end of 4 1/2" x 7" fabric to toilet paper roll. This will make it easier for children to cover the roll. Attach 8" square fabric to styrofoam ball with a few drops of glue. Gather fabric around ball to form the shepherd's head covering and secure with the rubber band.) Pull fabric around roll and glue. Glue on arms and hands. Glue twig (shepherd's crook) to hand. Draw eyes and mouth on face. Put a ring of glue around the top of roll and press head on. Let dry.

Keys to Happiness

CHILDREN WILL

connect dots to reveal a message
read message
decorate keys

MATERIALS

2 large cardboard keys for each child; markers; glue; glitter; brushes

PROCEDURE

(Teacher preparation: In dots that the children can connect, print I'M SORRY on half the keys and I FORGIVE on the other half. Give every child 1 of each key. Tell the children they will be happy if they remember to do what is written on the keys.) Connect the dots and read the messages. Decorate the keys with markers. Paint with a solution of watered down white glue. Quickly sprinkle glitter on keys. Take home and hang on your wall.

Love Chain

CHILDREN WILL

cut out and decorate love chain
read "I'm sorry" and "I forgive"
express personal sorrow and forgiveness

MATERIALS

Markers; glue; scissors; for each child: 4" x 14" paper; 2 paper clips; 2 small "I forgive" labels; 2 small "I'm sorry" labels

Pattern for Good Shepherd

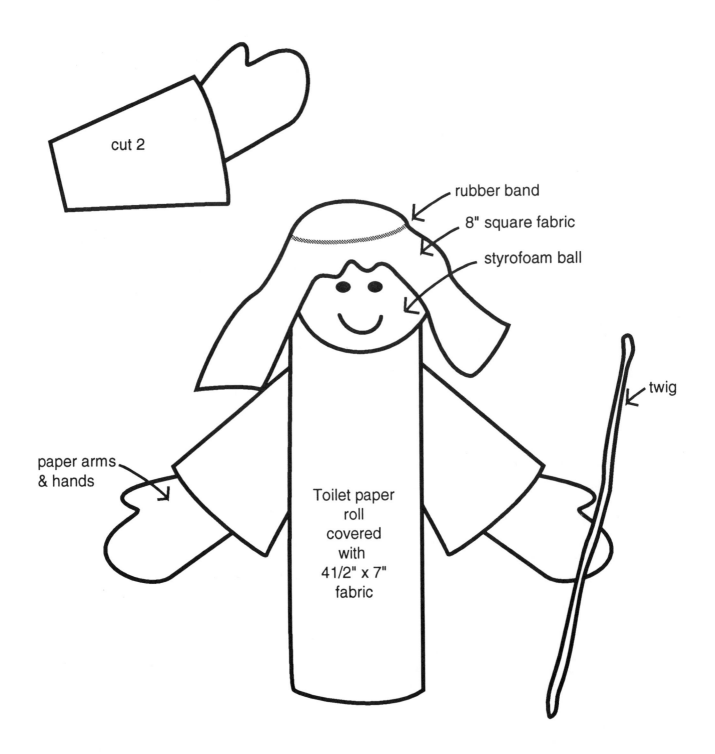

cut 2

rubber band

8" square fabric

styrofoam ball

twig

paper arms & hands

Toilet paper roll covered with 41/2" x 7" fabric

PROCEDURE

(Teacher preparation: Fold paper, accordian style, to make four 4" x 3 1/2" sections. Draw a heart on the top section, leaving a 1 1/2" space at the folds. Paper clip at the folds.) Cut out heart through all the sections, being careful to leave attached at the folds. Remove paper clips. Open chain. Glue 1 label on each heart. Decorate. Take home. Cut apart and give to someone to say "I'm sorry" or "I forgive."

Forgiveness Booklet

CHILDREN WILL

draw happy and sad faces

see a sad face become happy

describe how unkindness and forgiveness makes them feel

identify personal examples of unkindness and forgiveness

MATERIALS

Markers; glue; stapler; for each child: 8 1/2" x 11" construction paper; 8 1/2" x 5 1/2" construction paper

PROCEDURE

(Teacher preparation: At top of 8 1/2" x 11" paper, print WHEN I AM; at bottom of same paper, print FORGIVEN, I FEEL [blank]. At bottom of smaller paper, print UNKIND, I FEEL [blank]. Draw a large oval on the 8 1/2" x 11" paper. Staple the smaller paper to the bottom half of the larger. Complete the oval on the smaller sheet.) Print SAD in the first blank. Draw a frown on the face. Open the booklet. Print GLAD in the second blank. Draw a smile on the face. Read the booklet and give examples.

Forgiveness Booklet

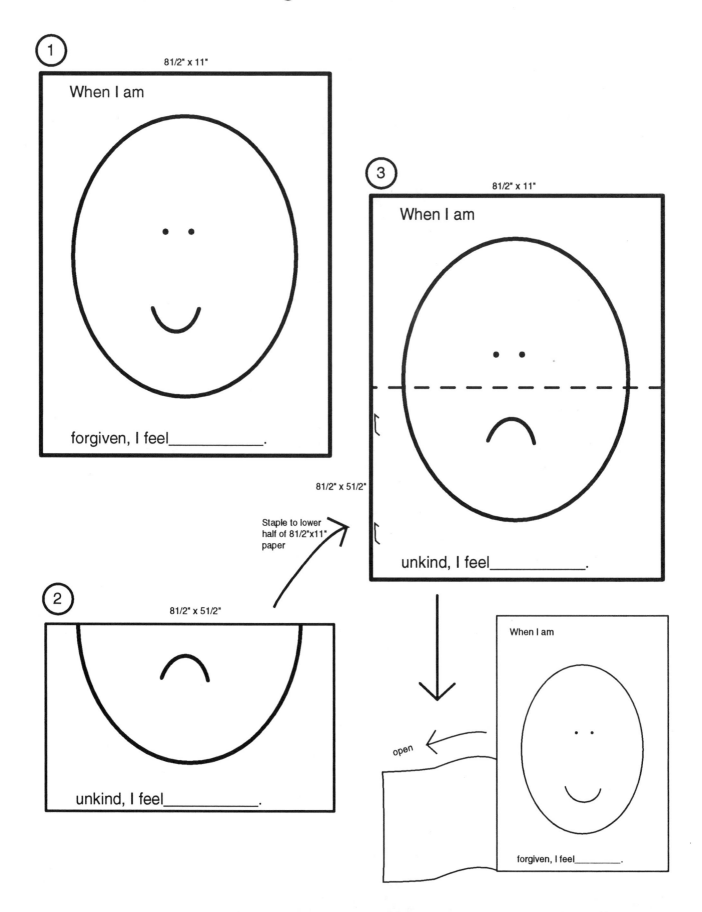

Movement

Sad Can Be Glad
PROCEDURE

Count off by 2's. 1's and 2's face each other. Say the following chant and do the appropriate motions:

All: Sad *(frown)* can be glad *(smile)* when you say,
1's: I'm sorry.
All: Sad *(frown)* can be glad *(smile)* when you say,
2's: I forgive.
All: Sad *(frown)* can be glad *(smile)* when you say,
1's: I still like you.
All: Sad *(frown)* can be glad *(smile)* when you say,
2's: We're still friends.
(All shake hands.)

Sorry/Forgive Mix-up
MATERIALS

For half the children: armbands that have a broken heart and the word, "sorry"; for half the children: armbands that have a heart and the words, "I forgive"; cassette tape of "Peace Time"

PROCEDURE

All those wearing "sorry" armbands make a circle at one side of the room. Those wearing "I forgive" armbands make a circle at the other side of the room. Walk around your circle to the music of "Peace Time." When the music stops, those with "sorry" armbands move around the room saying "Sorry!" until they find someone with an "I forgive" armband. Tap that person on the shoulder. The person will respond "I forgive," and the 2 become partners and sit in the center of the room. After everyone finds a partner, return to your circle and start again. Try to find a different partner each time.

Sorry Puppet
MATERIALS

Hand puppet; box of cards describing hurtful situations, i.e., "You tripped me," "You wouldn't take turns," "You called me a bad name," "You hit me," "You took my crayon," etc.

PROCEDURE

Work in pairs. 1 child moves and speaks for the puppet. The other child chooses a card and reads it, directing the dialogue to the puppet. The puppet verbalizes being sorry. The reader verbalizes forgiveness. The puppet and reader hug. Switch roles. Give all children a turn to verbalize sorrow and forgiveness.

Search for Forgiveness

MATERIALS

4 hand-sized cardboard keys

PROCEDURE

(Teacher preparation: Print I'M SORRY on 2 keys and I FORGIVE on 2 keys.) 2 people are "it." They each take an "I'm sorry" key and leave the room. The other children sit in a large circle. 2 take "I forgive" keys and hide them in their pockets, up their sleeves, or under their legs. The "I'm sorry's" come in and have 30 seconds to find forgiveness. They do this by tapping someone on the shoulder and saying "I'm sorry." When they tap someone who is hiding an "I forgive" key, that person must say "I forgive" and show the key. When both keys have been found, the "I'm sorry's" give their keys to 2 others who leave the room. The "I forgive's" give their keys to 2 others who hide them and the game continues until all have had a turn.

Prayer

Prayer Activity

MATERIALS:

Lamb- and shepherd-stick puppets (hand-drawn or cut from greeting cards or clip-art books); for each child: 35 mm. film case, decorated with lamb stickers and containing an important message. (See below.)

PROCEDURE:

Sit in a circle. Watch the puppets and listen as the teacher says,

Once a little lamb ran away. It got lost. It was sad and frightened. The shepherd loved the lamb. The shepherd was sad because the lamb was gone. The shepherd looked and looked for the lamb. Finally, the shepherd found the lamb. The shepherd was happy! "I'm sorry," said the lamb. "I forgive you," said the shepherd. The lamb was happy, too!

Jesus is like the shepherd. He loves us and takes care of us. We are like the lamb. Sometimes we do things that make people sad. But we don't have to stay sad. Here's how we can be happy again. (Open the film case and look at message as teacher reads.) "When we say we are sorry, Jesus always forgives us and makes us feel happy again." Let's all say "Thank you, Jesus." Take your message home and share it with someone.

RESPONSE PRAYER

Teacher: Loving God, when we feel left out,
Children: help us to forgive.
Teacher: When someone is mean to us,
Children: help us to forgive.
Teacher: When someone makes fun of us,
Children: help us to forgive.
All: Thank you for forgiving us.

REPEAT PRAYER

PROCEDURE

Children repeat after teacher:
Loving God,/ help us to say "I'm sorry"/ when we make people sad./ Thank you for/ forgiving us/ and making us feel glad./ Amen.

Music

Hi, God! 27260.
   (North American Liturgy Resources, 2110 W. Peoria Ave., Phoenix, AZ 85029).
   "Peace Time"

Hi, God 2. 27262.
   (North American Liturgy Resources, 2110 W. Peoria Ave., Phoenix, AZ 80529).
   "Jesus, Jesus"
   "Peace is Flowing Like a River"
   "What Shall I Do?"

Holy House. 6120.
   (World Library Publications, Inc., 5040 N. Ravenswood, Chicago, IL 60640).
   "Peace Chant"

The Music Machine. BWR 2004.
   (Sparrow Records, 8587 Canoga Ave., Canoga Park, CA 91304).
   "Kindness"

Watch With Me/Joe Wise. 28189.
   (North American Liturgy Resources, 2110 W. Peoria Ave., Phoenix, AZ 85029).
   "Go Now in Peace"

Books

Aliki. *Feelings*. New York: Mulberry Books, 1984.

Berenstain, Jan and Stan. *Berenstain Bears Get in a Fight*. New York: Random House, 1982.

Berry, Joy Wilt. *Let's Talk About Fighting*. Chicago: Children's Press, 1984.

Cohen, Miriam. *Best Friends*. New York: Macmillan, 1971.

Dragonwood, Crescent. *I Hate My Brother Harry*. New York: Harper & Row, 1983.

Hazen, Barbara Shook. *Even If I Did Something Awful*. New York: Atheneum, 1981.

Hoban, Russell. *Tom and the Two Handles*. New York: Harper & Row, 1965.

Hoban, Russell and Lillian. *The Sorely Trying Day*. New York: Harper & Row, 1964.

Kellogg, Steven. *Island of the Skog*. New York: Dial Books, 1973.

Mayer, Mercer and Marianna. *One Frog Too Many*. New York: Dial Press, 1975.

Riehecky, Janet. *"I'm Sorry."* Chicago: Children's Press, 1989.

Riley, Susan. *What Does It Mean, Sorry?* Elgin, Ill.: Child's World, 1978.

Sharmat, Marjorie. *I'm Not Oscar's Friend Anymore*. New York: E.P. Dutton, 1975.

Sharmat, Marjorie. *Sometimes Mama and Papa Fight*. New York: Harper & Row, 1980.

Stevenson, James. *Are We Almost There?* New York: Greenwillow Books, 1985.

Udry, Janice. *Let's Be Enemies*. New York: Harper & Row, 1961.

Wilhelm, Hans. *Let's Be Friends Again*. New York: Crown Publishers, 1986.

Winthrop, Elizabeth. *Katherine's Doll*. New York: E.P. Dutton, 1983.

Zolotow, Charlotte. *The Hating Book*. New York: Harper & Row, 1969.

Zolotow, Charlotte. *The Quarreling Book*. New York: Harper & Row, 1963.

Parent Page

Ideas for things to do for and with your child and family to nurture forgiveness:

Smile.
Be patient.
Accept an apology without saying "I told you so."
Say "I'm sorry" when you are wrong.
Invite a friend who's been unkind to come to your house.
Take a walk together. Hold hands and don't talk.
Read a story about forgiveness.
Talk about feelings: your own and your child's.
Present a flower to say "I'm sorry."
Bake Forgiveness Cupcakes. (Put a red candy heart in the center.)
Tell your child the story of the Prodigal Son.
Help the person you've forgiven to do a chore.
Sit quietly together. Listen to music, watch the rain, or look at the stars.
Let a teddy bear help someone say, "I'm sorry."
Say "Let's be friends again," and really mean it.
Pray together. Tell God how you feel.
Take the phone off the hook, shut off the TV and let everyone prepare and
   share an "It's-a-brand-new-day breakfast" to celebrate forgiveness.
Hold a family pow-wow and talk about grievances and ways to work them
   out.
Insist that family members say "I'm sorry" for any offensive acts, and "I for-
   give" when an apology is offered.
Give a hug to everyone in your family every day.

**"Be kind to one another, tender-hearted, forgiving one another,
just as God has forgiven you in Christ. "**— Ephesians 4:32

CHAPTER 9

Praying

Discussion

BACKGROUND

Communication is a necessary part of every relationship, and so prayer, our communication with God, is essential if we want to know God. We help children develop their relationship with God by helping them feel comfortable talking and listening to God.

Encouraging and modeling spontaneous prayer fosters this feeling of comfort.

Teach children that they can talk to God any time and any place by praying simple prayers as they work and play. Give praise for a butterfly, a brightly colored leaf, a child's good idea. Tell God when you feel sad or disappointed and ask for help.

Make opportunities to pray in many different ways. Pray while sitting, kneeling, or standing, with arms raised, hands folded, or holding hands. Speak, sing, or think a prayer. Write, dance, or paint a prayer. Pray all together by having the children repeat lines after you or saying a response in unison. Pray individually by taking turns to complete a prayer or make up personal prayers. Sit quietly and feel God's presence as you focus on a wonder of nature or listen to music.

Use the Bible often. Hold it as you read several verses or paraphrase a story. Keep the Bible in a special place that is accessible to the children.

QUESTIONS

When can you talk to God?

Where can you talk to God?

What can you talk to God about?

What are some things God made? Do you think God did a good job?

What do we tell someone who does a good job? (It's good to praise God.)

Who did God make all these gifts for?

What do we say when someone gives us something? (It's good to thank God.)

When we do something wrong, why is it good to tell God we're sorry?

When do you ask God for help?

Discovery Centers

Holy Card Matching

CHILDREN WILL

    sort and match pictures

    become familiar with saints

    become familiar with Christian art

MATERIALS

    2 each of 12 different holy cards

PROCEDURE

    (Teacher preparation: mix up cards.) Sort cards and match. Mix up when you are finished so someone else can have a turn.

Prayer Puzzles

CHILDREN WILL

    put puzzles together

    read prayers

    become familiar with 4 types of prayer

MATERIALS

    Short prayers printed on 9" x 12" posterboard: (DEAR GOD, YOU ARE WONDERFUL; DEAR GOD, I'M SORRY; DEAR GOD, PLEASE HELP ME; DEAR GOD, THANK YOU); clear contact paper

PROCEDURE

    (Teacher preparation: Cover prayers with contact paper. Cut apart to make puzzle pieces.) Put puzzles together. Read the prayer.

Rosary Bead Match

CHILDREN WILL

    see pictures of the joyful mysteries

    handle beads

    match beads to pictures

    become familiar with events in Jesus' life

MATERIALS

    1 picture of each of the joyful mysteries, each in a paper frame of a different color; 5 egg box bottoms, cut to have 10 spaces; container with 50 beads, 10 of each color to correspond with paper frames

PROCEDURE

    (Teacher preparation: Label each of the pictures, i.e., "An angel talks to Mary," "Mary visits her cousin Elizabeth," "Jesus is born," "Jesus is blessed in the temple," "Mary and Joseph find Jesus.") Choose a bead. Match its color to the color of a frame. Say the name of the picture in that frame. Place the bead in the container in front of that picture.

Song of Daniel Matching Game

CHILDREN WILL

compare and match texts
read blessings from Daniel
see that all creation praises the Lord
become familiar with some Hebrew Scriptures

MATERIALS

15 sheets of construction paper; markers; magazines

PROCEDURE

(Teacher preparation: Choose 10 blessings from Daniel 3:62-82. Print one blessing on each of 10 pieces of construction paper, i.e., SUN AND MOON, BLESS THE LORD, etc. Draw or glue a picture to illustrate each blessing. Cut the remaining 5 sheets of paper in half. Copy the blessings and drawings from the large sheets onto the half sheets. Underline or color code the first letters on the pairs.) Take 1 of the small cards. Match it to the blessing on one of the large cards. Read the blessing.

Telephone Prayer

CHILDREN WILL

use a telephone to "call" God
practice talking to God
make up spontaneous prayers

MATERIALS

Toy telephones or discarded telephones

PROCEDURE

Pretend you are calling God. Tell God how you feel today. Thank God for something or ask for some help.

Crafts

Soap Prayer Book

CHILDREN WILL

    pin ribbon; glue felt

    make a symbolic prayer book

    make a gift

MATERIALS

    For each child: 1 bar of soap, 3" x 2" x $3/4$"; felt, 5" x 3 $1/4$"; yellow or gold ribbon, $3/4$" x 7 $1/2$"; 2 straight pins; 1 sticker (Jesus or a cross); glue

PROCEDURE

    Position ribbon around soap to make page edges. Secure by pinning to "spine" $3/4$" from top and bottom. Glue felt to large, flat surfaces of soap, forming the cover. Glue sticker to the front. (Note: This makes a nice gift for someone who is sick or shut in.)

Telephone Prayer Book

CHILDREN WILL

    complete prayer sentences

    pray the 4 types of prayer

    assemble a prayer book

    be reminded that God always listens

    share prayers

MATERIALS

    Markers; stapler; glue; for each child: construction paper telephone; 4 telephone-shaped pieces of typing paper, 3 white paper (1 $1/2$") squares

PROCEDURE

    (Teacher preparation: Print GOD ALWAYS LISTENS across the telephone receiver. Print a prayer sentence to be completed on each page of the 4-page set: THANK YOU, GOD, FOR *[blank]*; WHEN I DO SOMETHING WRONG, I SAY, DEAR GOD, I'M *[blank]*. DEAR GOD, PLEASE HELP *[blank]*. WOW, GOD, YOU MADE A WONDERFUL *[blank]*. Print G, O, D on the white squares.) Glue these to the phone for push buttons. Complete the prayer sentences. Staple phone cover and prayer pages together. Share prayers.

Come, Little Children Plaque

CHILDREN WILL

    see pictures of children from different countries

    choose, arrange, and glue pictures

    make a picture showing Jesus surrounded by children

    read a Bible verse

Soap Prayer Book

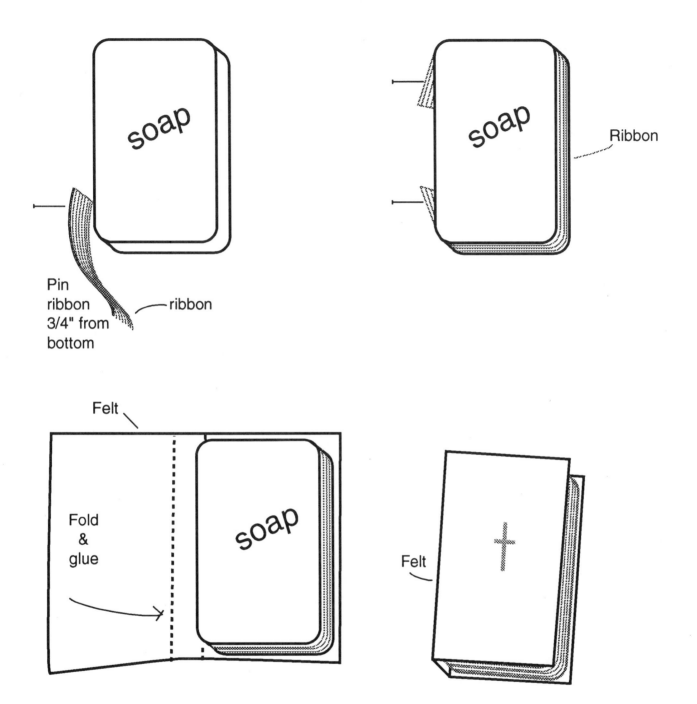

Pin
ribbon
3/4" from
bottom

ribbon

Ribbon

Felt

Fold
&
glue

soap

Felt

MATERIALS

Markers; glue; scissors; for each child: a picture of Jesus; several pictures of children from different lands; 8" x 10" white posterboard; 2" x 10" posterboard

PROCEDURE

(Teacher preparation: At bottom of posterboard, print LET THE CHILDREN COME TO ME [Mark 10:14].) Choose and glue a picture of Jesus to the posterboard. Choose pictures of children. Glue them around Jesus. Draw a background. Fold 2" x 10" posterboard in half. Cut 2 slits at the top, midway between the fold and edge. Stand plaque in slits.

Bible Bookmarks

CHILDREN WILL

hear short Bible verses
choose and decorate a Bible verse
sew cover on verse
make a useful object

MATERIALS

Variety of 2" x 6" cards with short Bible verses, i.e., "Love one another, as I have loved you" (John 15:12), "Be kind to one another" (Ephesians 4:32), "The Lord is my shepherd" (Psalm 23:1), etc.; stickers; for each child: two $2\,3/4$" x $6\,3/4$" plastic rectangles with holes punched around the perimeter; 36" yarn with 1 end covered with tape

PROCEDURE

(Teacher preparation: Read verses to children.) Choose a Bible verse. Decorate with stickers. Sandwich verse between plastic rectangles. Whip stitch yarn through holes and tie together at top.

Movement

Prayer Stretch

The Lord is in the heavens! *(reach way up high)*
The Lord is in the seas! *(make rippling movement with hands)*
The Lord is on the mountain tops *(raise hands over head; form a point)*
And the deep valleys! *(bring point down to sweep the ground)*
The Lord is in the sunlight! *(hands high; trace sunbeams falling to Earth)*
The Lord is in the air! *(spread fingers, move arms through space)*
The Lord is all around me *(extend arms to sides, turn around)*
God is ev-ery-where! *(extend hands to side, palms up, slowly raise them)*

Musical Prayer Game

MATERIALS

Large ball; cassette tape of "Make a Joyful Noise"

PROCEDURE

Sit in a circle. Play "Make a Joyful Noise." Pass the ball around the circle. When the music stops, the person holding the ball says a short prayer, i.e., "I love you, God," "Thank you, God, for kittens," etc. Give everyone a turn to pray.

Sometimes When I Pray

PROCEDURE

Do appropriate motions as you say this verse:

Sometimes when I pray I kneel *(kneel)*
    and tell God just how I feel.
Sometimes when I pray I stand *(stand)*
    very tall and fold my hands. *(fold hands)*
Sometimes when I pray I sing,
    "Thank you, God, for everything!" *(sing this line)*

Creature Dance

PROCEDURE

Tell the children that all creatures praise God. Ask them to think of an animal, then pantomime how that animal would move as it praised God. The other children must guess what the animal is. Give everyone a turn.

Hoo-ray March

PROCEDURE

March, clap, or beat time on home made instruments as you sing (tune: "When the Saints Go Marching In"):

Hoo-ray for God! Hoo-ray for God!

Hoo-ray for God who cares for me!
Oh, I'm glad my God is a loving God;
Hoo-ray for God who cares for me!

Prayer Finger Play

PROCEDURE
Show appropriate number of fingers as you sing (tune: "Ten Little Indians"):

I say: 1 little, 2 little, 3 little prayers,
4 little, 5 little, 6 little prayers,
7 little, 8 little, 9 little prayers,
10 little prayers to God.

God hears: 1 little, 2 little, 3 little prayers,
4 little, 5 little, 6 little prayers,
7 little, 8 little, 9 little prayers,
10 little prayers of mine.

Prayer

Prayer Activity

MATERIALS

Globe; pictures of children from around the world; cassette tape of "He's Got the Whole World in His Hands"

PROCEDURE

Sit in a circle around the globe. Tell the children: "God made Earth and all living things. God loves everything that was made: you and all the children who live all around the world. Let's look at some of the children God loves." Show pictures and name the country the children are from as you play "He's Got the Whole World." Then say, "God also loves *(name each of the children in your group)*." Ask the children to stand, hold hands, and circle the globe as you all sing one chorus of "He's Got the Whole World." Pray in unison, "God bless us everyone!"

RESPONSE PRAYER

Teacher: Loving God, we don't need a special place or time to talk with you, because you always hear us. When we are resting,

Children: we can talk to you.

Teacher: When we are playing,

Children: we can talk to you.

Teacher: When we are waiting,

Children: we can talk to you.

Teacher: When we are working,

Children: we can talk to you.

REPEAT PRAYER

PROCEDURE

Children repeat after teacher:

Loving God,/ I like to talk with you./ Thank you for listening./ Help me to/ listen to you./ Amen.

Music

Bullfrogs and Butterflies. BWR 2010.
     (Sparrow Records, 8587 Canoga Ave., Canoga Park, CA. 91304).
     "My Hands Belong to You"

Hi, God! 27260.
     (North American Liturgy Resources, 2110 W. Peoria Ave., Phoenix, AZ 85029).
     "Come and Go With Me to My Father's House"
     "Father, We Adore You"
     "Sing a Simple Song"

Kids Praise! 2. MM0078A.
     (Maranatha Music, P.O. Box 1396, Costa Mesa, CA 92626).
     "In His Time"
     "Lord, Be Glorified"
     "Make a Joyful Noise"

Kids Praise! 5. SPCN-7-100-14282-2.
     (Maranatha Music, P.O. Box 1396, Costa Mesa, CA 92626).
     "God Is Great"

Mahalia Jackson Sings America's Favorite Hymns. CGK 30744.
     (Columbia Records, 51 W. 52nd St., New York, NY 10019).
     "He's Got the Whole World in His Hands"

Books

Baynes, Pauline. *Thanks Be to God*. New York: Macmillan, 1990.
Bishop, Roma, illust. *A Little Book of Prayers*. Boston: Little, Brown & Co., 1987.

Caswell, Helen. *I Can Talk with God*. Nashville: Abingdon Press, 1989.
Costello, Gwen. *Praying with Children*. Mystic, Conn.: Twenty-Third Publications, 1990.

Francis of Assisi. *Song of the Sun*. New York: Macmillan, 1952.

Goble, Paul. *I Sing for the Animals*. New York: Bradbury Press, 1991.

Hague, Michael. *A Child's Book of Prayers*. New York: Holt, Rinehart & Winston, 1985.
Harmer, Juliet. *Prayers for Children*. New York: Viking Press, 1990.
Haywood, Carolyn. *Make a Joyful Noise!* Philadelphia: Westminster Press, 1984.

Jones, Jessie. *This Is the Way*. New York: Viking Press, 1951.

Kaufman, William. *UNICEF Book of Children's Prayers*. Harrisburg, Pa.: Stackpole Books, 1970.

Larrick, Nancy. *Tambourines! Tambourines to Glory!* Philadelphia: Westminster Press, 1982.

Magagna, Anna Marie. *First Prayers*. New York: Macmillan, 1982.
Mitchell, Cynthia. *Here a Little Child I Stand*. New York: Philomel Books, 1985.

Royds, Caroline. *Prayers for Little Children*. New York: Doubleday, 1988.

Titherington, Jeanne. *A Child's Prayer*. New York: Greenwillow Books, 1989.

Watson, Carol. *365 Children's Prayers*. Oxford: Leon Publishing, 1989.
Wilkin, Eloise. illust. *Prayers for a Small Child*. New York: Random House, 1984.
Wilkin, Eloise. *Songs of Praise*. New York: American Heritage Press, 1970.
Wilkin, Esther. *The Golden Treasury of Prayers for Boys and Girls*. New York: Golden Press, 1975.

Parent Page

Ideas for things to do for and with your child and family to nurture the love of prayer:

Each day, make the sign of the cross on your child's forehead and say, "God bless you."

Teach your child to make the sign of the cross.

Hang a crucifix in your home.

Take turns giving thanks before meals.

Attend Mass together.

Keep a Bible where all can reach it.

Let your child see you pray.

Go to a prayer service, such as Evening Song, together.

Give your child a rosary to hold as the family prays it together.

Go to the public library and choose a colorful children's prayer book.

Make a prayer table. Pick wildflowers to decorate it.

Read stories of the saints.

Sit quietly and listen to God in the sound of the wind, the ocean, the rustling of leaves, the song of a bird.

Light a candle at church and pray together.

Place a religious picture or statue in your child's room.

Kneel with your child at bedtime and pray together.

Sing a song of prayer together.

Take a walk and share a spontaneous prayer of praise for something you see.

Help your child write his or her own prayer.

Pray together for those who are sick or need help. Send a card, phone them, deliver some food, or visit with them.

"Prayer makes the heart grow until it is able to contain God."

— Mother Teresa

CHAPTER 10   LOVING GOD'S WORLD

Discussion

BACKGROUND

Everything God made tells us something about God. As we explore and discover creation, we learn more about God. The closer we feel to the things God made, the closer we will feel to God. Those who see God in all of creation will view everything as sacred and will want to be good stewards of God's gifts.

Children's natural curiosity is a most valuable asset as they explore God's many gifts. To a child, everything is full of wonder: a wiggly worm, moss on a tree, a dandelion. A child takes time to see, to watch, to wonder, to admire. But in order for this wonder to survive, says Rachel Carson in *A Sense of Wonder*, the child needs to share it with an adult. Unfortunately, we adults have a tendency to look and not really see. We need to slow down and let our children and students teach us to see the world through "new" eyes so that we can share and support their wonder. Then we can gently lead them to feel and articulate appreciation and thanks for all of God's gifts.

Give children many opportunities and plenty of time to observe, touch, hear, smell, taste God's wonderful world. Share in the enjoyment of their discoveries. Invite them to praise God joyfully, spontaneously, and with a thankful heart.

QUESTIONS

What is the most beautiful thing God made?

What colors are in it? What shape is it? How does it feel?

What are some round things that God made?

What did God make that is good to eat? What do they taste like?

What is something God made that smells very nice?

What are some things God made that we need to live?

Who did God make all these wonderful things for?

What do we say to someone who gives us things?

What do you think God wants us to do with all these things?

Discovery Centers

Color Count

CHILDREN WILL

    observe autumn leaf with magnifying glass

    identify colors

MATERIALS

    Autumn leaves; magnifying glass; red, green, brown, yellow, orange, construction paper circles

PROCEDURE

    Choose a leaf. Study it carefully with the magnifying glass. Identify all the colors it contains by matching the corresponding circles of colors to it.

Texture Time

CHILDREN WILL

    feel textures

    sort items according to texture

MATERIALS

    Box containing natural items with a variety of textures; 2 trays, 1 labeled SMOOTH and 1 ROUGH

PROCEDURE

    Take an item out of the box. Feel. Place in the appropriate tray.

Water Magnifier

CHILDREN WILL

    choose objects to test

    observe magnifying property of water

MATERIALS

    1 empty 5-lb. peanut butter bucket; plastic wrap; rubber band; sharp knife; variety of small objects; water

PROCEDURE

    (Teacher preparation: Cut a circle, large enough for a child's hand to fit in, in the side of the container, near the bottom. Cover the top loosely with plastic wrap so that it sags a little. Secure plastic wrap with rubber band. Fill the plastic depression with water.) Choose an object. Place it in the container. Look at it through the water. Tell what happens.

Microscopic Topic

CHILDREN WILL
>
> observe natural item
>
> describe color, shape, pattern

MATERIALS
>
> Assortment of natural items, i.e., thin slice of carrot and beet, flower petal, etc., magnifying glass

PROCEDURE
>
> Choose an item. Study it closely with magnifying glass. Describe what you see.

Magnify Match

CHILDREN WILL
>
> observe parts of natural items with a magnifying glass
>
> match parts to whole item

MATERIALS
>
> 2 pairs of flowers; 2 pairs of vegetables or fruits; magnifying glass; 1 large tray; 4 paper plates

PROCEDURE
>
> (Teacher preparation: Break 1 of each item into its parts, i.e., stem, leaves, seeds, petals, etc. Mix up all the pieces and place on the tray. Put each whole object on a paper plate.) Choose something from the tray. Study it with the magnifying glass. Look at the whole object. Decide which one your piece came from. Put your piece with it.

Seed Sorter

CHILDREN WILL
>
> observe and touch 12 different kinds of seeds
>
> learn that seeds come in different shapes, colors, textures, sizes
>
> arrange seeds by size

MATERIALS
>
> Egg carton with a different seed in each space, i.e., large and small seeds from fruits, vegetables, flowers, and trees; large tray

PROCEDURE
>
> Study the seeds. Choose the smallest. Put it on the tray. Continue until you have arranged the seeds from the smallest to the largest.

Crafts

Evergreen Wreath

CHILDREN WILL
       feel and shape clay
       feel and smell evergreen pieces
       compare texture of evergreens and clay
       arrange evergreens in clay
       make an ornament

MATERIALS
       Self-hardening clay; 2" pieces of evergreen; ribbon

PROCEDURE
       Roll a lime-sized piece of clay into a snake. Attach ends to form a circle. Push evergreens into clay to make a wreath. Let dry. Tie on a ribbon loop for hanging.

Turtle Puppet

CHILDREN WILL
       trace, cut and glue turtle parts to body
       feel seeds
       make a nature toy

MATERIALS
       Green construction paper; pattern for head, legs, tail; scissors; glue; markers; stapler; dried pumpkin seeds; for each child: green paper cupcake liner; rubber band

PROCEDURE
       Trace and cut out turtle's head, 4 legs, and tail. Draw eyes and mouth on the head. Turn cupcake liner upside down. Glue head, legs, and tail to inside of liner at appropriate points and fold up. Turn turtle right side up. Glue seeds to flat part of liner to make shell. Cut rubber band in half. Staple each end to the sides of the turtle on the inside of the liner. Leaving your thumb free, slide the turtle onto your hand. Move your turtle around. (Note: Do motions for "The Little Turtle": *Collected Poems* by Vachel Lindsay, Macmillan Publishing Co., N.Y.)

Sunny Day Plate

CHILDREN WILL
       feel and observe dried plants
       identify things God made
       draw and arrange a nature scene
       make a sun catcher

Patterns for Turtle Puppet

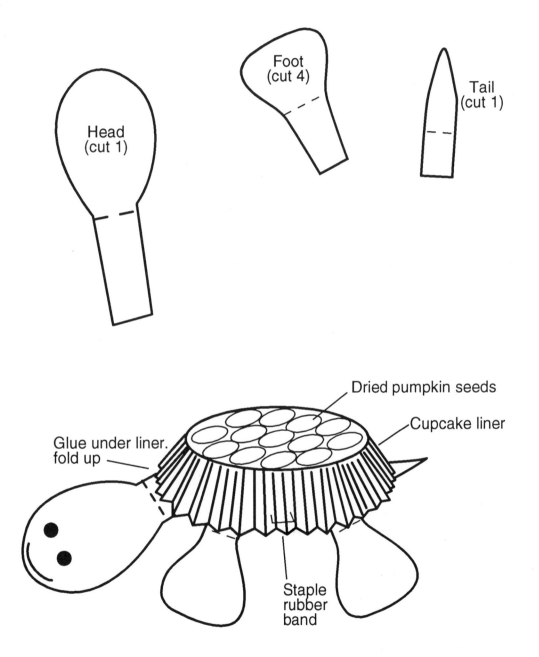

Head
(cut 1)

Foot
(cut 4)

Tail
(cut 1)

Dried pumpkin seeds

Cupcake liner

Glue under liner.
fold up

Staple
rubber
band

MATERIALS

Markers; glue; tape; dried plants; pre-cut pictures of animals and plants; for each child: paper plate; 3" square of yellow cellophane

PROCEDURE

(Teacher preparation: Cut a 2" diameter circle near the top of each plate.) Turn the plate to the back. Cover circle with cellophane and tape in place. Turn plate to the front. Draw in the sky and grass. Glue on dried plants and pre-cut pictures to complete a sunny day scene. Tape in a window and see the sunlight come through the cellophane.

Ocean Blue Plate

CHILDREN WILL

feel finger paint
mix colors
observe fish or see pictures of fish
copy patterns and colors of fish
share their creations with other children

MATERIALS

Blue and green finger paint; white paper fish shapes; markers; glue; pictures of brightly colored fish or an aquarium with tropical fish

PROCEDURE

Finger paint the ocean on your plate. Let dry. Choose fish shapes. Observe fish in aquarium or in pictures. Copy the patterns and colors onto your fish shapes. Arrange and glue the fish on your plate. Make an aquarium by displaying all the plates. Visit the aquarium and try to match the fish on the plates with the real fish or those in the pictures.

Movement

God's Gifts/Echo Pantomime

PROCEDURE

Children echo the teacher's words and motions after each line.

God made the water *(make rippling movement with hands)*,
The ground *(touch ground)*, and the sky *(reach up high)*,
The animals that walk *(let your fingers walk up your arm)*,
And the birds that fly *(flap arms)*,
The fish that swim *(swimming motion)*
In the blue, blue sea *(make rippling movement with hands)*,
The sun *(make large circle)*, and the moon *(small circle)*,
And you *(point to others)*, and me *(point to self)*!
Thank you, God, *(fold hands in prayer, extend upwards)*
For our gifts, big *(hands far apart)* and small *(hands close)*.
Help us, please, to share them all *(palms up, extend hands to others)*.

Find Blue Bug

MATERIALS

Blue Bug's Beach Party by Virginia Poulet; large brown grocery bag; ten 7" x 9" posterboard cards; 6 shoeboxes without lids; ball; 3 gum wrappers; 3 orange peels; 3 bottle caps; 3 straws; 2 crumpled napkins; 2 pieces of ripped newspaper; trash can; markers; tape

PROCEDURE

(Teacher preparation: Cut grocery bag to make a rectangle, about 36" x 18", to represent the beach. Draw a bag-sized "Blue Bug" on the beach. Tape a different kind of trash to the bottom of each shoe box. Tape 1 piece of the remaining trash to each card. Cover "Blue Bug" with the trash cards.) Form 2 groups, "Rollers" and "Finders." The first "Roller" rolls the ball into one of the boxes and chooses a "Finder" to find the same kind of trash on the beach. The "Finder" picks up 1 piece of matching trash and puts it in the trash can. The next "Roller" rolls. The game continues until "Blue Bug" is found. Play again, reversing roles.

Don't Waste a Drop

MATERIALS

Yardstick; 4 oz. paper cup, half full of water

PROCEDURE

Tell the children to pretend there is only 1/2 cup of clean water left for everyone to drink. Their mission is to take the water to someone who is very thirsty. (No one will really drink the water.) To do this, they must successfully cross a log (the yardstick) without falling off or spilling any water. Their orders are, "Don't

---

waste a drop!" Form 2 groups. Make a line at opposite ends of the yardstick. Take turns carrying the water, relay style, to the person waiting at the opposite end of the log. Cheer together for successful deliveries. Celebrate the completed mission with a drink of cool water.

Alphabet Water Cheer

PROCEDURE

Alternate stooping with hands on hips and standing as you stretch up high while shouting this cheer:

Stoop: A,B,C,D,E,F,G!
Stretch: Everything needs water, we all agree!
Stoop: H, I, J, K, L, M, N, O, P!
Stretch: Tigers, and giraffes, and the bumble bee!
Stoop: Q, R, S! — T, U, V!
Stretch: Dolphins that swim way under the sea!
Stoop: W, X! — Y and Z!
Stretch: Puppies and cats and you and me!
Clap: For giving us water, God, we thank thee!

Prayer

Prayer Activity

MATERIALS

Nature items the children have brought from home; partially wrapped gift boxes; gift tags that say "To: Everyone/From: God"; tape

PROCEDURE

Children put their nature item in a gift box, tape it shut, and attach a tag. Place the gifts around the prayer table.

Teacher: God gives us many gifts and wants us to share them all. Let's do that now.
(Give each child a gift, making sure no one receives what he [she] brought.)
Teacher: Look at the wonderful things God gives us to share. Let's thank God for the gifts. Thank you, God, for *(each child finishes the sentence, naming what he [she] has received.)*
All: Thank you, God, for all your gifts. Help us to share them with others.

RESPONSE PRAYER

Teacher: God made the sun and the stars.
Children: God is good.
Teacher: God made the land and the sea.
Children: God is good.
Teacher: God made the animals and the people.
Children: God is good.
Teacher: God made everything for you and for me.
Children: God is good.

REPEAT PRAYER

PROCEDURE

Children repeat after teacher:
Loving God,/ you made a beautiful world./ Help us to love it/ and take care of it./ Amen.

Music

Ella Jenkins: Come, Dance by the Ocean. SF 45014.
  (Folkways Records and Service Corp., 43 W. 61st St., New York, NY 10023).
  "Can't Sink a Rainbow"
  "Come, Dance by the Ocean"
  "Let's Not Waste the Food We Eat"
  "A Solution to Pollution"

Holy House. 6120.
  (World Library Publications, Inc., 5040 N. Ravenswood, Chicago, IL 60640).
  "Jubilee"

Kid's Praise! 2. MM0078A.
  (Maranatha Music, P. O. Box 1396, Costa Mesa, CA 92628).
  "Arky, Arky"

Kid's Praise! 5. SPCN-7-100-14282-2.
  (Maranatha Music, P. O. Box 1396, Costa Mesa, CA 92628.)
  "On a Starry Night"

Zany Zoo. HP-101.
  (Educational Activities, Box 392, Freeport, NY 11520).
  "Amazing"

Books

Aragon, Jane. *Salt Hands.* New York: E.P. Dutton, 1989.

Bester, Roger. *Guess What?* New York: Crown Publishers, 1980.
Blake, Robert. *The Perfect Spot.* New York: Philomel Books, 1992.
Brown, Marcia. *Walk With Your Eyes.* New York: Watts, 1979.

Ehlert, Lois. *Red Leaf, Yellow Leaf.* New York: Harcourt, Brace, Jovanovich, 1991.

Foreman, Michael. *One World.* Boston: Little, Brown, & Co., 1990.

Hoban, Julia. *Amy Loves the Sun.* New York: Harper & Row, 1988.
Hoban, Tana. *Look Again!* New York: Macmillan, 1971.

Kelly, Kathleen. *River Friends.* New York: Atheneum, 1988.

LeTord, Bijou. *The Deep Blue Sea.* New York: Orchard Books, 1990.
Lionni, Leo. *It's Mine!* New York: Alfred A. Knopf, 1986.

Parker, Steve. *Pond and River.* New York: Alfred A. Knopf, 1988.
Peters, Lisa. *Water's Way.* New York: Arcade, 1991.
Poulet, Virginia. *Blue Bug's Beach Party.* Chicago: Children's Press, 1975.

Schmid, Eleonore. *The Water's Journey.* New York: North-South Books, 1990.
Sheehan, Kathryn, and Mary Waidner. *Earth Child.* Tulsa: Council Oak Books, 1991.

Titherington, Jeanne. *Pumpkin, Pumpkin.* New York: Greenwillow Books, 1986.
Tresselt, Alvin. *The Gift of the Tree.* New York: Lothrop, Lee, & Shepard, 1972.

Wolf, Ashley. *A Year of Beasts.* New York: E. P. Dutton, 1986.
Wright, Dare. *Edith and Little Bear Lend a Hand.* New York: Random House, 1972.

Parent Page

Ideas for things to do with your child and family to nurture a love for God's world:

Take a walk in the rain on a warm day. See how many reasons you can think of to thank God for water.

Put a leaf in a stream. Follow it as it floats downstream.

Walk on dried leaves. Enjoy the crunching sound.

Lie on the ground. Describe the cloud pictures you see.

Sit quietly in a forest. Look. Listen. When you go home, describe how you felt, what you saw and heard.

Lie in the snow and make snow angels.

Watch a spider spinning its web. Look at dewdrops on the web in the early morning.

Walk on the beach in your bare feet. Let the waves wash your toes.

Catch a firefly. Tell it a secret. Let it go.

Take a night hike, or sleep outdoors. Identify night sounds.

Plant something you can eat. Water and weed it. Harvest it and share it with someone.

Watch the bees collect pollen. Close your eyes and listen to their sound.

Take off your shoes and walk on the rocks in a shallow stream.

Look for "rainbows" on the pavement after a rain. Count the colors you see.

Follow your child on a wonder-walk. Collect or stop and observe things your child wonders about.

Watch the sunrise or a sunset.

Stand outside. Close your eyes. Slowly turn and feel the wind. Tell what direction it is coming from.

Climb a hill or mountain. Look all around below you. Praise God for making Earth.

Look at the moon and the stars through a telescope.

Look at the snowflakes on your window with a magnifying glass.

"Come and see what marvels God has done!" — Psalm 66:5

Of Related Interest...

WHEN JESUS WAS YOUNG

Carole MacClennan

Helps children in grades K-5 understand the life and times of Jesus through activities such as grinding wheat for bread or weaving a mat.
ISBN: 0-89622-485-6, 80 pp, $7.95

ACTING OUT THE MIRACLES AND PARABLES

Sr. Mary Kathleen Glavich

52 playlets for the elementary grades that will enliven and enrich religion classes.
ISBN: 0-89622-363-9, 142 pages, $12.95

GOSPEL PLAYS FOR STUDENTS

36 Scripts for Education and Worship

Sr. Mary Kathleen Glavich

Favorite and less familiar Gospel events scripted in easy-to-understand language. For children of all ages.
ISBN: 0-89622-407-4, 112 pp, $12.95

TEACHING THE BIBLE WITH PUPPETS

Jeanne S. Fogle

Offers tips on puppet construction, staging, backdrops and musical accompaniment, plus 17 sample scripts.
ISBN: 0-89622-405-8, 80 pp, $9.95

Available at religious bookstores or from

TWENTY-THIRD PUBLICATIONS
P.O. Box 180
Mystic, CT 06355

1-800-321-0411